W9-CKT-577

CHRONICLES OF CANADA

Edited by George M. Wrong and H. H. Langton

In thirty-two volumes

11

THE WINNING OF CANADA

BY WILLIAM WOOD

Part III

The English Invasion

JAMES WOLFE

From the National Portrait Gallery

514.706

THE WINNING OF CANADA

A Chronicle of Wolfe

BY

WILLIAM WOOD

EX UNO
DISCE OMNES

TORONTO
GLASGOW, BROOK & COMPANY
1915

THE LIBRARY
COLBY JUNIOR COLLEGE
NEW LONDON, N. H.

F
1003
C56
vol. 11

*Copyright in all Countries subscribing to
the Berne Convention*

13905

TO

MY MOTHER

AUTHOR'S NOTE

ANY life of Wolfe can be artificially simplified by treating his purely military work as something complete in itself and not as a part of a greater whole. But, since such treatment gives a totally false idea of his achievement, this little sketch, drawn straight from original sources, tries to show him as he really was, a co-worker with the British fleet in a war based entirely on naval strategy and inseparably connected with international affairs of world-wide significance. The only simplification attempted here is that of arrangement and expression.

W. W.

Quebec, April 1914.

CONTENTS

ILLUSTRATIONS

CHAPTER I

THE BOY

1727-1741

WOLFE was a soldier born. Many of his ancestors had stood ready to fight for king and country at a moment's notice. His father fought under the great Duke of Marlborough in the war against France at the beginning of the eighteenth century. His grandfather, his great-grandfather, his only uncle, and his only brother were soldiers too. Nor has the martial spirit deserted the descendants of the Wolfes in the generation now alive. They are soldiers still. The present head of the family, who represented it at the celebration of the tercentenary of the founding of Quebec, fought in Egypt for Queen Victoria; and the member of it who represented Wolfe on that occasion, in the pageant of the Quebec campaign, is an officer in the Canadian army under George V.

The Wolfes are of an old and honourable

line. Many hundreds of years ago their fore-fathers lived in England and later on in Wales. Later still, in the fifteenth century, before America was discovered, they were living in Ireland. Wolfe's father, however, was born in England; and, as there is no evidence that any of his ancestors in Ireland had married other than English Protestants, and as Wolfe's mother was also English, we may say that the victor of Quebec was a pure-bred Englishman. Among his Anglo-Irish kinsmen were the Goldsmiths and the Seymours. Oliver Goldsmith himself was always very proud of being a cousin of the man who took Quebec.

Wolfe's mother, to whom he owed a great deal of his genius, was a descendant of two good families in Yorkshire. She was eighteen years younger than his father, and was very tall and handsome. Wolfe thought there was no one like her. When he was a colonel, and had been through the wars and at court, he still believed she was ' a match for all the beauties.' He was not lucky enough to take after her in looks, except in her one weak feature, a cutaway chin. His body, indeed, seems to have been made up of the bad points of both parents: he had his rheumatism from his father. But his spirit was made up of all their good points ; and no braver ever lived in any healthy body than in his own sickly, lanky six foot three.

Wolfe's parents went to live at Westerham in Kent shortly after they were married ; and there, on January 2, 1727, in the vicarage— where Mrs Wolfe was staying while her husband was away on duty with his regiment—the victor of Quebec was born. Two other houses in the little country town of Westerham are full of memories of Wolfe. One of these was his father's, a house more than two hundred years old when he was born. It was built in the reign of Henry VII, and the loyal subject who built it had the king's coat of arms carved over the big stone fireplace. Here Wolfe and his younger brother Edward used to sit in the winter evenings with their mother, while their veteran father told them the story of his long campaigns. So, curiously enough, it appears that Wolfe, the soldier who won Canada for England in 1759, sat under the arms of the king in whose service the sailor Cabot hoisted the flag of England over Canadian soil in 1497. This house has been called Quebec House ever since the victory in 1759. The other house is Squerryes Court, belonging

then and now to the Warde family, the Wolfes'
closest friends.   Wolfe and George Warde were
chums from the first day they met.   Both
wished to go into the Army; and both, of
course, 'played soldiers,' like other virile
boys.   Warde lived to be an old man and
actually did become a famous cavalry leader.
Perhaps when he charged a real enemy, sword
in hand, at the head of thundering squadrons,
it may have flashed through his mind how he
and Wolfe had waved their whips and cheered
like mad when they galloped their ponies down
the common with nothing but their barking
dogs behind them.

Wolfe's parents presently moved to Greenwich, where he was sent to school at Swinden's.
Here he worked quietly enough till just before
he entered on his 'teens.   Then the long-pent
rage of England suddenly burst in war with
Spain.   The people went wild when the British
fleet took Porto Bello, a Spanish port in Central
America.   The news was cried through the
streets all night.   The noise of battle seemed to
be sounding all round Swinden's school, where
most of the boys belonged to naval and military
families.   Ships were fitting out in English har-
bours.   Soldiers were marching into every

English camp. Crowds were singing and cheering. First one boy's father and then another's was under orders for the front. Among them was Wolfe's father, who was made adjutant-general to the forces assembling in the Isle of Wight. What were history and geography and mathematics now, when a whole nation was afoot to fight! And who would not fight the Spaniards when they cut off British sailors' ears? That was an old tale by this time; but the flames of anger threw it into lurid relief once more.

Wolfe was determined to go and fight. Nothing could stop him. There was no commission for him as an officer. Never mind! He would go as a volunteer and win his commission in the field. So, one hot day in July 1740, the lanky, red-haired boy of thirteen-and-a-half took his seat on the Portsmouth coach beside his father, the veteran soldier of fifty-five. His mother was a woman of much too fine a spirit to grudge anything for the service of her country; but she could not help being exceptionally anxious about the dangers of disease for a sickly boy in a far-off land of pestilence and fever. She had written to him the very day he left. But he, full of the stir and excitement of a big camp, had carried the letter in his pocket for two or three days before answering it. Then he wrote her the first of many letters from different seats of war, the last one of all being written just before he won the victory that made him famous round the world.

Newport, Isle of Wight,
August 6th, 1740.

I received my dearest Mamma's letter on Monday last, but could not answer it then, by reason I was at camp to see the regiments off to go on board, and was too late for the post ; but am very sorry, dear Mamma, that you doubt my love, which I 'm sure is as sincere as ever any son's was to his mother.

Papa and I are just going on board, but I believe shall not sail this fortnight ; in which time, if I can get ashore at Portsmouth or any other town, I will certainly write to you, and, when we are gone, by every ship we meet, because I know it is my duty. Besides, if it is not, I would do it out of love, with pleasure.

I am sorry to hear that your head is so bad, which I fear is caused by your being so melancholy ; but pray, dear Mamma, if

you love me, don't give yourself up to fears
for us. I hope, if it please God, we shall
soon see one another, which will be the
happiest day that ever I shall see. I will,
as sure as I live, if it is possible for me, let
you know everything that has happened,
by every ship; therefore pray, dearest
Mamma, don't doubt about it. I am in a
very good state of health, and am likely
to continue so. Pray my love to my
brother. Pray my service to Mr Streton
and his family, to Mr and Mrs Weston, and
to George Warde when you see him; and
pray believe me to be, my dearest Mamma,
your most dutiful, loving and affectionate
son,   J. Wolfe.

To Mrs. Wolfe, at her house in Greenwich, Kent.

Wolfe's ' very good state of health ' was not
' likely to continue so,' either in camp or on
board ship. A long peace had made the
country indifferent to the welfare of the Army
and Navy. Now men were suddenly being
massed together in camps and fleets as if on
purpose to breed disease. Sanitation on a
large scale, never having been practised in
peace, could not be improvised in this hurried,
though disastrously slow, preparation for a

war. The ship in which Wolfe was to sail had been lying idle for years; and her pestilential bilge-water soon began to make the sailors and soldiers sicken and die. Most fortunately, Wolfe was among the first to take ill; and so he was sent home in time to save him from the fevers of Spanish America.

Wolfe was happy to see his mother again, to have his pony to ride and his dogs to play with. But, though he tried his best to stick to his lessons, his heart was wild for the war. He and George Warde used to go every day during the Christmas holidays behind the pigeon-house at Squerryes Court and practise with their swords and pistols. One day they stopped when they heard the post-horn blowing at the gate; and both of them became very much excited when George's father came out himself with a big official envelope marked 'On His Majesty's Service' and addressed to 'James Wolfe, Esquire.' Inside was a commission as second lieutenant in the Marines, signed by George II and dated at St James's Palace, November 3, 1741. Eighteen years later, when the fame of the conquest of Canada was the talk of the kingdom, the Wardes had a stone monument built to mark the spot where Wolfe was standing when the squire handed him his first commission. And there it is to-day; and on it are the verses ending,

> This spot so sacred will forever claim
> A proud alliance with its hero's name.

Wolfe was at last an officer. But the Marines were not the corps for him. Their service companies were five thousand miles away, while war with France was breaking out much nearer home. So what was his delight at receiving another commission, on March 25, 1742, as an ensign in the 12th Regiment of Foot! He was now fifteen, an officer, a soldier born and bred, eager to serve his country, and just appointed to a regiment ordered to the front! Within a month an army such as no one had seen since the days of Marlborough had been assembled at Blackheath. Infantry, cavalry, artillery, and engineers, they were all there when King George II, the Prince of Wales, and the Duke of Cumberland came down to review them. Little did anybody think that the tall, eager ensign carrying the colours of the 12th past His Majesty was the man who was to play the foremost part in winning Canada for the British crown.

CHAPTER II

THE YOUNG SOLDIER

1741-1748

WOLFE'S short life may be divided into four periods, all easy to remember, because all are connected with the same number—seven. He was fourteen years a boy at home, with one attempt to be a soldier. This period lasted from 1727 to 1741. Then he was seven years a young officer in time of war, from 1741 to 1748. Then he served seven years more in time of peace, from 1748 to 1755. Lastly, he died in the middle, at the very climax, of the world-famous Seven Years' War, in 1759.

After the royal review at Blackheath in the spring of 1742 the army marched down to Deptford and embarked for Flanders. Wolfe was now off to the very places he had heard his father tell about again and again. The surly Flemings were still the same as when his father knew them. They hated their

British allies almost as much as they hated their enemies. The long column of redcoats marched through a scowling mob of citizens, who meanly grudged a night's lodging to the very men coming there to fight for them. We may be sure that Wolfe thought little enough of such mean people as he stepped out with the colours flying above his head. The army halted at Ghent, an ancient city, famous for its trade and wealth, and defended by walls which had once resisted Marlborough.

At first there was a good deal to do and see ; and George Warde was there too, as an officer in a cavalry regiment. But Warde had to march away ; and Wolfe was left without any companion of his own age, to pass his spare time the best way he could. Like another famous soldier, Frederick the Great, who first won his fame in this very war, he was fond of music and took lessons on the flute. He also did his best to improve his French ; and when Warde came back the two friends used to go to the French theatre. Wolfe put his French to other use as well, and read all the military books he could find time for. He always kept his kit ready to pack; so that he could have marched anywhere within two hours of receiving the order. And, though only a mere boy-officer, he began to learn the duties of an adjutant, so that he might be fit for promotion whenever the chance should come.

Months wore on and Wolfe was still at Ghent. He had made friends during his stay, and he tells his mother in September : ' This place is full of officers, and we never want company. I go to the play once or twice a week, and talk a little with the ladies, who are very civil and speak French.' Before Christmas it had been decided at home—where the war-worn father now was, after a horrible campaign at Cartagena—that Edward, the younger son, was also to be allowed to join the Army. Wolfe was delighted. ' My brother is much to be commended for the pains he takes to improve himself. I hope to see him soon in Flanders, when, in all probability, before next year is over, we may know something of our trade.' And so they did !

The two brothers marched for the Rhine early in 1743, both in the same regiment. James was now sixteen, Edward fifteen. The march was a terrible one for such delicate boys. The roads were ankle-deep in mud ; the weather was vile ; both food and water were very bad. Even the dauntless Wolfe had to confess to his mother that he was ' very much fatigued and out of order. I never come into quarters without aching hips and knees.' Edward, still more delicate, was sent off on a foraging party to find something for the regiment to eat. He wrote home to his father from Bonn on April 7: ' We can get nothing upon our march but eggs and bacon and sour bread. I have no bedding, nor can get it anywhere. We had a sad march last Monday in the morning. I was obliged to walk up to my knees in snow, though my brother and I have a horse between us. I have often lain upon straw, and should oftener, had I not known some French, which I find very useful ; though I was obliged the other day to speak *Latin* for a good dinner. We send for everything we want to the priest.'

That summer, when the king arrived with his son the Duke of Cumberland, the British and Hanoverian army was reduced to 37,000 half-fed men. Worse still, the old general, Lord Stair, had led it into a very bad place. These 37,000 men were cooped up on the narrow side of the valley of the river Main, while a much larger French army was on the better side, holding bridges by which to cut them off and attack them while they were all clumped together. Stair tried to slip away in the night.

But the French, hearing of this attempt, sent 12,000 men across the river to hold the place the British general was leaving, and 30,000 more, under the Duc de Gramont, to block the road at the place towards which he was evidently marching. At daylight the British and Hanoverians found themselves cut off, both front and rear, while a third French force was waiting to pounce on whichever end showed weakness first. The King of England, who was also Elector of Hanover, would be a great prize, and the French were eager to capture him. This was how the armies faced each other on the morning of June 27, 1743, at Dettingen, the last battle-field on which any king of England has fought in person, and the first for Wolfe.

The two young brothers were now about to see a big battle, like those of which their father used to tell them. Strangely enough, Amherst, the future commander-in-chief in America, under whom Wolfe served at Louisbourg, and the two men who succeeded Wolfe in command at Quebec—Monckton and Townshend—were also there. It is an awful moment for a young soldier, the one before his first great fight. And here were nearly a hundred thousand men, all in full view of each

other, and all waiting for the word to begin.
It was a beautiful day, and the sun shone down
on a splendidly martial sight.   There stood the
British and Hanoverians, with wooded hills on
their right, the river and the French on their
left, the French in their rear, and the French
very strongly posted on the rising ground
straight in their front.   The redcoats were in
dense columns, their bayonets flashing and
their colours waving defiance.   Side by side
with their own red cavalry were the black
German cuirassiers, the blue German lancers,
and the gaily dressed green and scarlet
Hungarian hussars.   The long white lines of
the three French armies, varied with royal blue,
encircled them on three sides.   On the fourth
were the leafy green hills.

Wolfe was acting as adjutant and helping
the major.   His regiment had neither colonel
nor lieutenant-colonel with it that day; so
he had plenty to do, riding up and down to see
that all ranks understood the order that they
were not to fire till they were close to the
French and were given the word for a volley.
He cast a glance at his brother, standing
straight and proudly with the regimental
colours that he himself had carried past the
king at Blackheath the year before.   He was

not anxious about 'Ned'; he knew how all
the Wolfes could fight. He was not anxious
about himself; he was only too eager for the
fray. A first battle tries every man, and few
have not dry lips, tense nerves, and beating
hearts at its approach. But the great anxiety
of an officer going into action for the first
time with untried men is for them and not
for himself. The agony of wondering whether
they will do well or not is worse, a thousand
times, than what he fears for his own safety.

Presently the French gunners, in the centre
of their position across the Main, lit their
matches and, at a given signal, fired a salvo
into the British rear. Most of the baggage
wagons were there ; and, as the shot and shell
began to knock them over, the drivers were
seized with a panic. Cutting the traces, these
men galloped off up the hills and into the woods
as hard as they could go. Now battery after
battery began to thunder, and the fire grew hot
all round. The king had been in the rear,
as he did not wish to change the command
on the eve of the battle. But, seeing the panic,
he galloped through the whole of his army to
show that he was going to fight beside his men.
As he passed, and the men saw what he intended to do, they cheered and cheered, and

took heart so boldly that it was hard work to keep them from rushing up the heights of Dettingen, where Gramont's 30,000 Frenchmen were waiting to shoot them down.

Across the river Marshal Noailles, the French commander-in-chief, saw the sudden stir in the British ranks, heard the roaring hurrahs, and supposed that his enemies were going to be fairly caught against Gramont in front. In this event he could finish their defeat himself by an overwhelming attack in flank. Both his own and Gramont's artillery now redoubled their fire, till the British could hardly stand it. But then, to the rage and despair of Noailles, Gramont's men, thinking the day was theirs, suddenly left their strong position and charged down on to the same level as the British, who were only too pleased to meet them there. The king, seeing what a happy turn things were taking, galloped along the front of his army, waving his sword and calling out, 'Now, boys! Now for the honour of England!' His horse, maddened by the din, plunged and reared, and would have run away with him, straight in among the French, if a young officer called Trapaud had not seized the reins. The king then dismounted and put himself at the head of his troops, where he remained fighting, sword in hand, till the battle was over.

Wolfe and his major rode along the line of their regiment for the last time. There was not a minute to lose. Down came the Royal Musketeers of France, full gallop, smash through the Scots Fusiliers and into the line in rear, where most of them were unhorsed and killed. Next, both sides advanced their cavalry, but without advantage to either. Then, with a clear front once more, the main bodies of the French and British infantry rushed together for a fight to a finish. Nearly all of Wolfe's regiment were new to war and too excited to hold their fire. When they were within range, and had halted for a moment to steady the ranks, they brought their muskets down to the ' present.' The French fell flat on their faces and the bullets whistled harmlessly over them. Then they sprang to their feet and poured in a steady volley while the British were reloading. But the second British volley went home. When the two enemies closed on each other with the bayonet, like the meeting of two stormy seas, the British fought with such fury that the French ranks were broken. Soon the long white waves rolled back and the long red waves rolled forward. Dettingen was reached and the desperate fight was won.

Both the boy-officers wrote home, Edward to his mother, James to his father. Here is a part of Edward's letter :

My brother and self escaped in the engagement and, thank God, are as well as ever we were in our lives, after not only being cannonaded two hours and three-quarters, and fighting with small arms [muskets and bayonets] two hours and one-quarter, but lay the two following nights upon our arms ; whilst it rained for about twenty hours in the same time, yet are ready and as capable to do the same again. The Duke of Cumberland behaved charmingly. Our regiment has got a great deal of honour, for we were in the middle of the first line, and in the greatest danger. My brother has wrote to my father and I believe has given him a small account of the battle, so I hope you will excuse it me.

A manly and soldier-like letter for a boy of fifteen ! Wolfe's own is much longer and full of touches that show how cool and observant

he was, even in his first battle and at the age of
only sixteen. Here is some of it :

The Gens d'Armes, or Mousquetaires
Gris, attacked the first line, composed of
nine regiments of English foot, and four or
five of Austrians, and some Hanoverians.
But before they got to the second line, out
of two hundred there were not forty living.
These unhappy men were of the first
families in France. Nothing, I believe,
could be more rash than their undertaking.
The third and last attack was made by the
foot on both sides. We advanced towards
one another ; our men in high spirits, and
very impatient for fighting, being elated
with beating the French Horse, part of
which advanced towards us ; while the
rest attacked our Horse, but were soon
driven back by the great fire we gave them.
The major and I (for we had neither colonel
nor lieutenant-colonel), before they came
near, were employed in begging and ordering
the men not to fire at too great a distance, but to keep it till the enemy should
come near us ; but to little purpose. The
whole fired when they thought they could
reach them, which had like to have ruined

us. However, we soon rallied again, and attacked them with great fury, which gained us a complete victory, and forced the enemy to retire in great haste. We got the sad news of the death of as good and brave a man as any amongst us, General Clayton. His death gave us all sorrow, so great was the opinion we had of him. He had, 'tis said, orders for pursuing the enemy, and if we had followed them, they would not have repassed the Main with half their number. Their loss is computed to be between six and seven thousand men, and ours three thousand. His Majesty was in the midst of the fight ; and the duke be- haved as bravely as a man could do. I had several times the honour of speaking with him just as the battle began and was often afraid of his being dashed to pieces by the cannon-balls. He gave his orders with a great deal of calmness and seemed quite unconcerned. The soldiers were in high delight to have him so near them. I some- times thought I had lost poor Ned when I saw arms, legs, and heads beat off close by him. A horse I rid of the colonel's, at the first attack, was shot in one of his hinder legs and threw me ; so I was obliged to do the duty of an adjutant all that and the next day on foot, in a pair of heavy boots. Three days after the battle I got the horse again, and he is almost well.

Shortly after Dettingen Wolfe was appointed adjutant and promoted to a lieutenancy. In the next year he was made a captain in the 4th Foot while his brother became a lieutenant in the 12th. After this they had very few chances of meeting; and Edward, who had caught a deadly chill, died alone in Flanders, not yet seventeen years old. Wolfe wrote home to his mother:

Poor Ned wanted nothing but the satisfaction of seeing his dearest friends to leave the world with the greatest tranquillity. It gives me many uneasy hours when I reflect on the possibility there was of my being with him before he died. God knows it was not apprehending the danger the poor fellow was in; and even that would not have hindered it had I received the physician's first letter. I know you won't be able to read this without shedding tears, as I do writing it. Though it is the custom of the army to sell the deceased's effects, I could not suffer it. We none of us want, and I thought the best way would be to bestow them on the deserving whom he had an esteem for in his lifetime. To his servant—the most honest and faithful man I ever knew—I gave all his clothes. I gave his horse to his friend Parry. I know he loved Parry, and for that reason the horse will be taken care of. His other horse I keep myself. I have his watch, sash, gorget, books, and maps, which I shall preserve to his memory. He was an honest and good lad, had lived very well, and always discharged his duty with the cheerfulness becoming a good officer. He lived and died as a son of you two should. There was no part of his life that makes him dearer to me than what you so often mentioned—*he pined after me.*

It was this pining to follow Wolfe to the wars that cost poor Ned his life. But did not Wolfe himself pine to follow his father?

The next year, 1745, the Young Pretender, ' Bonnie Prince Charlie,' raised the Highland clans on behalf of his father, won several battles, and invaded England, in the hope of putting the Hanoverian Georges off the throne

of Great Britain and regaining it for the exiled
Stuarts. The Duke of Cumberland was sent
to crush him ; and with the duke went Wolfe.
Prince Charlie's army retreated and was at
last brought to bay on Culloden Moor, six miles
from Inverness. The Highlanders were not
in good spirits after their long retreat before
the duke's army, which enjoyed an immense
advantage in having a fleet following it along
the coast with plenty of provisions, while the
prince's wretched army was half starved.
We may be sure the lesson was not lost on
Wolfe. Nobody understood better than he
that the fleet is the first thing to consider in
every British war. And nobody saw a better
example of this than he did afterwards in
Canada.

At daybreak on April 16, 1746, the Highlanders found the duke's army marching
towards Inverness, and drew up in order to
prevent it. Both armies halted, each hoping
the other would make the mistake of charging.
At last, about one o'clock, the Highlanders in
the centre and right could be held back no
longer. So eager were they to get at the redcoats that most of them threw down their
muskets without even firing them, and then
rushed on furiously, sword in hand. ''Twas

for a time,' said Wolfe, ' a dispute between the swords and bayonets, but the latter was found by far the most destructable [*sic*] weapon.' No quarter was given or taken on either side during an hour of desperate fighting hand to hand. By that time the steady ranks of the redcoats, aided by the cavalry, had killed five times as many as they had lost by the wild slashing of the claymores. The Highlanders turned and fled. The Stuart cause was lost for ever.

Again another year of fighting : this time in Holland, where the British, Dutch, and Austrians under the Duke of Cumberland met the French at the village of Laffeldt, on June 21, 1747. Wolfe was now a brigade-major, which gave him the same sort of position in a brigade of three battalions as an adjutant has in a single one ; that is, he was a smart junior officer picked out to help the brigadier in command by seeing that orders were obeyed. The fight was furious. As fast as the British infantry drove back one French brigade another came forward and drove the British back. The village was taken and lost, lost and taken, over and over again. Wolfe, though wounded, kept up the fight. At last a new French brigade

charged in and swept the British out altogether.
Then the duke ordered the Dutch and Austrians
to advance. But the Dutch cavalry, right in
the centre, were seized with a sudden panic
and galloped back, knocking over their own
men on the way, and making a gap that certainly looked fatal. But the right man was
ready to fill it. This was Sir John Ligonier,
afterwards commander-in-chief of the British
Army at the time of Wolfe's campaigns in
Canada. He led the few British and Austrian
cavalry, among them the famous Scots Greys,
straight into the gap and on against the dense
masses of the French beyond. These gallant
horsemen were doomed; and of course they
knew it when they dashed themselves to death
against such overwhelming odds. But they
gained the few precious moments that were
needed. The gap closed up behind them; and
the army was saved, though they were lost.

During the day Wolfe was several times in
great danger. He was thanked by the duke in
person for the splendid way in which he had
done his duty. The royal favour, however, did
not make him forget the gallant conduct of
his faithful servant, Roland : ' He came to me
at the hazard of his life with offers of his
service, took off my cloak and brought a fresh

horse ; and would have continued close by me had I not ordered him to retire. I believe he was slightly wounded just at that time. Many a time has he pitched my tent and made the bed ready to receive me, half-dead with fatigue.' Nor did Wolfe forget his dumb friends : ' I have sold my poor little gray mare. I lamed her by accident, and thought it better to dismiss her the service immediately. I grieved at parting with so faithful a servant, and have the comfort to know she is in good hands, will be very well fed, and taken care of in her latter days.'

After recovering from a slight wound received at Laffeldt Wolfe was allowed to return to England, where he remained for the winter. On the morrow of New Year's Day, 1748, he celebrated his coming of age at his father's town house in Old Burlington Street, London. In the spring, however, he was ordered to rejoin the army, and was stationed with the troops who were guarding the Dutch frontier. The war came to an end in the same year, and Wolfe went home. Though then only twenty-one, he was already an experienced soldier, a rising officer, and a marked man.

CHAPTER III

THE SEVEN YEARS' PEACE

1748-1755

WOLFE was made welcome in England wherever he went. In spite of his youth his name was well known to the chief men in the Army, and he was already a hero among the friends of his family. By nature he was fond of the society of ladies, and of course he fell in love. He had had a few flirtations before, like most other soldiers ; but this time the case was serious. The difference was the same as between a sham fight and a battle. His choice fell on Elizabeth Lawson, a maid of honour to the Princess of Wales. The oftener he saw her the more he fell in love with her. But the course of true love did not, as we shall presently see, run any more smoothly for him than it has for many another famous man.

In 1749, when Wolfe was only twenty-two, he was promoted major of the 20th Regiment of Foot. He joined it in Scotland, where he was to serve for the next few years. At first he was not very happy in Glasgow. He did not like the people, as they were very different from the friends with whom he had grown up. Yet his loneliness only added to his zeal for study. He had left school when still very young, and he now found himself ignorant of much that he wished to know. As a man of the world he had found plenty of gaps in his general knowledge. Writing to his friend Captain Rickson, he says: ' When a man leaves his studies at fifteen, he will never be justly called a man of letters. I am endeavouring to repair the damages of my education, and have a person to teach me Latin and mathematics.' From his experience in his own profession, also, he had learned a good deal. In a letter to his father he points out what excellent chances soldiers have to see the vivid side of many things: ' That variety incident to a military life gives our profession some advantages over those of a more even nature. We have all our passions and affections aroused and exercised, many of which must have wanted their proper employment had not suitable occasions obliged us to exert them. Few men know their own courage till danger proves them, or how far

the love of honour or dread of shame are
superior to the love of life. This is a knowledge
to be best acquired in an army; our actions
are there in presence of the world, to be fully
censured or approved.'

Great commanders are always keen to learn
everything really worth while. It is only
the little men who find it a bore. Of course,
there are plenty of little men in a regiment,
as there are everywhere else in the world;
and some of the officers were afraid Wolfe
would insist on their doing as he did. But he
never preached. He only set the example,
and those who had the sense could follow
it. One of his captains wrote home: ' Our
acting colonel here is a paragon. He neither
drinks, curses, nor gambles. So we make him
our pattern.' After a year with him the
officers found him a ' jolly good fellow ' as
well as a pattern; and when he became their
lieutenant-colonel at twenty-three they gave
him a dinner that showed he was a prime
favourite among them. He was certainly
quite as popular with the men. Indeed, he
soon became known by a name which speaks
for itself—' the soldier's friend.'

By and by Wolfe's regiment marched
into the Highlands, where he had fought

against Prince Charlie in the '45. But he
kept in touch with what was going on in
the world outside. He wrote to Rickson
at Halifax, to find out for him all he could
about the French and British colonies in
America. In the same letter, written in 1751,
he said he should like to see some Highland
soldiers raised for the king's army and sent
out there to fight. Eight years later he was
to have a Highland regiment among his own
army at Quebec. Other themes filled the
letters to his mother. Perhaps he was thinking of Miss Lawson when he wrote : ' I have
a certain turn of mind that favours matrimony
prodigiously. I love children. Two or three
manly sons are a present to the world, and the
father that offers them sees with satisfaction
that he is to live in his successors.' He was
thinking more gravely of a still higher thing
when he wrote on his twenty-fifth birthday,
January 2, 1752, to reassure his mother about
the strength of his religion.

Later on in the year, having secured leave
of absence, he wrote to his mother in the
best of spirits. He asked her to look after all
the little things he wished to have done. ' Mr
Pattison sends a pointer to Blackheath ; if you
will order him to be tied up in your stable, it

will oblige me much. If you hear of a servant who can dress a wig it will be a favour done me to engage him. I have another favour to beg of you and you 'll think it an odd one : 'tis to order some currant jelly to be made in a crock for my use. It is the custom in Scotland to eat it in the morning with bread.' Then he proposed to have a shooting-lodge in the Highlands, long before any other Englishman seems to have thought of what is now so common. ' You know what a whimsical sort of person I am. Nothing pleases me now but hunting, shooting, and fishing. I have distant notions of taking a very little house, remote upon the edge of the forest, merely for sport.'

In July he left the Highlands, which were then, in some ways, as wild as Labrador is now. About this time there was a map made by a Frenchman in Paris which gave all the chief places in the Lowlands quite rightly, but left the north of Scotland blank, with the words ' Unknown land here, inhabited by the "Iglandaires" ! ' When his leave began Wolfe went first to Dublin—' dear, dirty Dublin,' as it used to be called—where his uncle, Major Walter Wolfe, was living. He wrote to his father : ' The streets are crowded with people of a large size and well limbed,

and the women very handsome. They have
clearer skins, and fairer complexions than the
women in England or Scotland, and are ex-
ceeding straight and well made'; which
shows that he had the proper soldier's eye for
every pretty girl. Then he went to London
and visited his parents in their new house at
the corner of Greenwich Park, which stands
to-day very much the same as it was then.
But, wishing to travel, he succeeded, after a
great deal of trouble, in getting leave to go to
Paris. Lord Bury was a friend of his, and Lord
Bury's father, the Earl of Albemarle, was the
British ambassador there. So he had a good
chance of seeing the best of everything. Perhaps it would be almost as true to say that he
had as good a chance of seeing the worst of
everything. For there were a great many
corrupt and corrupting men and women at
the French court. There was also much
misery in France, and both the corruption and
the misery were soon to trouble New France,
as Canada was then called, even more than
they troubled Old France at home.

Wolfe wished to travel about freely, to see
the French armies at work, and then to go
on to Prussia to see how Frederick the Great
managed his perfectly disciplined army. This

THE LIBRARY 13905
COLBY JUNIOR COLLEGE
NEW LONDON, N. H.

would have been an excellent thing to do.
But it was then a very new thing for an officer
to ask leave to study foreign armies. Moreover,
the chief men in the British Army did not like
the idea of letting such a good colonel go away
from his regiment for a year, even though he
was going with the object of making himself
a still better officer. Perhaps, too, his friends
were just a little afraid that he might join the
Prussians or the Austrians ; for it was not, in
those days, a very strange thing to join the
army of a friendly foreign country. Whatever the reason, the long leave was refused
and he went no farther than Paris.

Louis XV was then at the height of his
apparent greatness ; and France was a great
country, as it is still. But king and government were both corrupt. Wolfe saw this well
enough and remembered it when the next
war broke out. There was a brilliant society
in ' the capital of civilization,' as the people
of Paris proudly called their city ; and there
was a great deal to see. Nor was all of it
bad. He wrote home two days after his
arrival.

The packet [ferry] did not sail that night,
but we embarked at half-an-hour after six

in the morning and got into Calais at ten. I never suffered so much in so short a time at sea. The people [in Paris] seem to be very sprightly. The buildings are very magnificent, far surpassing any we have in London. Mr Selwin has recommended a French master to me, and in a few days I begin to ride in the Academy, but must dance and fence in my own lodgings. Lord Albemarle [the British ambassador] is come from Fontainebleau. I have very good reason to be pleased with the reception I met with. The best amusement for strangers in Paris is the Opera, and the next is the playhouse. The theatre is a school to acquire the French language, for which reason I frequent it more than the other.

In Paris he met young Philip Stanhope, the boy to whom the Earl of Chesterfield wrote his celebrated letters; 'but,' says Wolfe, 'I fancy he is infinitely inferior to his father.' Keeping fit, as we call it nowadays, seems to have been Wolfe's first object. He took the same care of himself as the Japanese officers did in the Russo-Japanese War; and for the same reason, that he might be the better able

to serve his country well the next time she
needed him.   Writing to his mother he says:

I am up every morning at or before
seven and fully employed till twelve.   Then
I dress and visit, and dine at two.   At five
most people go to the public entertainments, which keep you till nine; and at
eleven I am always in bed.   This way of
living is directly opposite to the practice
of the place.   But no constitution could
go through all.   Four or five days in the
week I am up six hours before any other
fine gentleman in Paris.   I ride, fence,
dance, and have a master to teach me
French.   I succeed much better in fencing
and riding than in the art of dancing, for
they suit my genius better; and I improve
a little in French.   I have no great ac-
quaintance with the French women, nor
am likely to have.   It is almost impossible
to introduce one's self among them without losing a great deal of money, which
you know I can't afford; besides, these
entertainments begin at the time I go to
bed, and I have not health enough to sit
up all night and work all day.   The people
here use umbrellas to defend them from

the sun, and something of the same kind
to secure them from the rain and snow.
I wonder a practice so useful is not introduced into England.

While in Paris Wolfe was asked if he would
care to be military tutor to the Duke of
Richmond, or, if not, whether he knew of any
good officer whom he could recommend. On
this he named Guy Carleton, who became the
young duke's tutor. Three men afterwards
well known in Canada were thus brought
together long before any of them became celebrated. The Duke of Richmond went into
Wolfe's regiment. The next duke became a
governor-general of Canada, as Guy Carleton
had been before him. And Wolfe—well, he
was Wolfe!

One day he was presented to King Louis,
from whom, seven years later, he was to
wrest Quebec. 'They were all very gracious
as far as courtesies, bows, and smiles go,
for the Bourbons seldom speak to anybody.'
Then he was presented to the clever Marquise
de Pompadour, whom he found having her
hair done up in the way which is still known
by her name to every woman in the world.
It was the regular custom of that time for

great ladies to receive their friends while the barbers were at work on their hair. 'She is extremely handsome and, by her conversation with the ambassador, I judge she must have a great deal of wit and understanding.' But it was her court intrigues and her shameless waste of money that helped to ruin France and Canada.

In the midst of all these gaieties Wolfe never forgot the mother whom he thought 'a match for all the beauties.' He sent her 'two black laced hoods and a *vestale* for the neck, such as the Queen of France wears.' Nor did he forget the much humbler people who looked upon him as 'the soldier's friend.' He tells his mother that his letters from Scotland have just arrived, and that 'the women of the regiment take it into their heads to write to me sometimes.' Here is one of their letters, marked on the outside, 'The Petition of Anne White':

Collonnell,—Being a True Noble-hearted Pittyful gentleman and Officer your Worship will excuse these few Lines concerning ye husband of ye under-signed, Sergt. White, who not from his own fault is not behaving as Hee should

towards me and his family, although good
and faithfull till the middle of November
last.

We may be sure 'Sergt. White' had to behave
'as Hee should' when Wolfe returned!

In April, to his intense disgust, Wolfe was
again in Glasgow.

> We are all sick, officers and soldiers.
> In two days we lost the skin off our faces
> with the sun, and the third were shivering
> in great coats. My cousin Goldsmith has
> sent me the finest young pointer that ever
> was seen; he eclipses Workie, and out-
> does all. He sent me a fishing-rod and
> wheel at the same time, of his own work-
> manship. This, with a salmon-rod from
> my uncle Wat, your flies, and my own
> guns, put me in a condition to undertake
> the Highland sport. We have plays, we
> have concerts, we have balls, with dinners
> and suppers of the most execrable food
> upon earth, and wine that approaches to
> poison. The men of Glasgow drink till
> they are excessively drunk. The ladies are
> cold to everything but a bagpipe—I wrong
> them—there is not one that does not melt
> away at the sound of money.'

By the end of this year, however, he had left Scotland for good. He did not like the country as he saw it. But the times were greatly against his doing so. Glasgow was not at all a pleasant place in those narrowly provincial days for any one who had seen much of the world. The Highlands were as bad. They were full of angry Jacobites, who could never forgive the redcoats for defeating Prince Charlie. Yet Wolfe was not against the Scots as a whole ; and we must never forget that he was the first to recommend the raising of those Highland regiments which have fought so nobly in every British war since the mighty one in which he fell.

During the next year and part of the year following, 1754-55, Wolfe was at Exeter, where the entertainments seem to have been more to his taste than those at Glasgow. A lady who knew him well at this time wrote : ' He was generally ambitious to gain a tall, graceful woman to be his partner, as well as a good dancer. He seemed emulous to display every kind of virtue and gallantry that would render him amiable.'

In 1755 the Seven Years' Peace was coming to an end in Europe. The shadow of the Seven Years' War was already falling darkly

across the prospect in America. Though
Wolfe did not leave for the front till 1757, he
was constantly receiving orders to be ready,
first for one place and then for another. So
early as February 18, 1755, he wrote to his
mother what he then thought might be a farewell letter. It is full of the great war ; but
personal affairs of the deeper kind were by no
means forgotten. ' The success of our fleet
in the beginning of the war is of the utmost
importance.' ' It will be sufficient comfort to
you both to reflect that the Power which has
hitherto preserved me may, if it be His pleasure,
continue to do so. If not, it is but a few
days more or less, and those who perish in
their duty and the service of their country
die honourably.'

The end of this letter is in a lighter vein.
But it is no less characteristic : it is all about
his dogs. ' You are to have Flurry instead of
Romp. The two puppies I must desire you to
keep a little longer. I can't part with either
of them, but must find good and secure quarters
for them as well as for my friend Cæsar, who
has great merit and much good humour. I
have given Sancho to Lord Howe, so that I am
reduced to two spaniels and one pointer.'
It is strange that in the many books about

dogs which mention the great men who have been fond of them—and most great men are fond of dogs—not one says a word about Wolfe. Yet ' my friend Cæsar, who has great merit and much good humour,' deserves to be remembered with his kind master just as much, in his way, as that other Cæsar, the friend of Edward VII, who followed his master to the grave among the kings and princes of a mourning world.

CHAPTER IV

THE SEVEN YEARS' WAR

1756-1763

WOLFE'S Quebec campaign marked the supreme
crisis of the greatest war the British Empire
ever waged : the war, indeed, that made the
Empire. To get a good, clear view of anything so vast, so complex, and so glorious, we
must first look at the whole course of British
history to see how it was that France and
England ever became such deadly rivals. It
is quite wrong to suppose that the French and
British were always enemies, though they have
often been called ' historic ' and ' hereditary '
foes, as if they never could make friends at
all. As a matter of fact, they have had many
more centuries of peace than of war ; and ever
since the battle of Waterloo, in 1815, they have
been growing friendlier year by year. But
this happy state of affairs is chiefly because,
as we now say, their ' vital interests no longer
clash '; that is, they do not both desire the

same thing so keenly that they have to fight for it.

Their vital interests do not clash now. But they did clash twice in the course of their history. The first time was when both governments wished to rule the same parts of the land of France. The second time was when they both wished to rule the same parts of the oversea world. Each time there was a long series of wars, which went on inevitably until one side had completely driven its rival from the field.

The first long series of wars took place chiefly in the fourteenth century and is known to history as the Hundred Years' War. England held, and was determined to hold, certain parts of France. France was determined never to rest till she had won them for herself. Whatever other things the two nations were supposed to be fighting about, this was always the one cause of strife that never changed and never could change till one side or other had definitely triumphed. France won. There were glorious English victories at Cressy and Agincourt. Edward III and Henry V were two of the greatest soldiers of any age. But, though the English often won the battles, the French won the war.

The French had many more men, they fought near their own homes, and, most important of all, the war was waged chiefly on land. The English had fewer men, they fought far away from their homes, and their ships could not help them much in the middle of the land, except by bringing over soldiers and food to the nearest coast. The end of it all was that the English armies were worn out; and the French armies, always able to raise more and more fresh men, drove them, step by step, out of the land completely.

The second long series of wars took place chiefly in the eighteenth century. These wars have never been given one general name ; but they should be called the Second Hundred Years' War, because that is what they really were. They were very different from the wars that made up the first Hundred Years' War, because this time the fight was for oversea dominions, not for land in Europe. Of course navies had a good deal to do with the first Hundred Years' War and armies with the second. But the navies were even more important in the second than the armies in the first. The Second Hundred Years' War, the one in which Wolfe did such a mighty deed, began with the fall of the Stuart kings of

England in 1688 and went on till the battle of
Waterloo in 1815. But the beginning and end
that meant most to the Empire were the naval
battles of La Hogue in 1692 and Trafalgar in
1805. Since Trafalgar the Empire has been
able to keep what it had won before, and to
go on growing as well, because all its different
parts are joined together by the sea, and because the British Navy has been, from that day
to this, stronger than any other navy in the
world.

How the French and British armies and
navies fought on opposite sides, either alone
or with allies, all over the world, from time
to time, for these hundred and twenty-seven
years; how all the eight wars with different
names formed one long Second Hundred
Years' War; and how the British Navy was
the principal force that won the whole of this
war, made the Empire, and gave Canada safety
then, as it gives her safety now—all this is
much too long a story to tell here. But the
gist of it may be told in a very few words, at
least in so far as it concerns the winning of
Canada and the deeds of Wolfe.

The name 'Greater Britain' is often used
to describe all the parts of the British Empire
which lie outside of the old mother country.

This ' Greater Britain ' is now so vast and well established that we are apt to forget those other empires beyond the seas which, each in its own day, surpassed the British Empire of the same period. There was a Greater Portugal, a Greater Spain, a Greater Holland, and a Greater France. France and Holland still have large oversea possessions ; and a whole new-world continent still speaks the languages of Spain and Portugal. But none of them has kept a growing empire oversea as their British rival has. What made the difference ? The two things that made all the difference in the world were freedom and sea-power. We cannot stop to discuss freedom, because that is more the affair of statesmen ; but, at the same time, we must not forget that the side on which Wolfe fought was the side of freedom. The point for us to notice here is that all the freedom and all the statesmen and all the soldiers put together could never have made a Greater Britain, especially against all those other rivals, unless Wolfe's side had also been the side of sea-power.

Now, sea-power means more than fighting power at sea ; it means trading power as well. But a nation cannot trade across the sea against its rivals if its own ships are captured and

theirs are not. And long before the Second
Hundred Years' War with France the other
sea-trading empires had been gradually giving
way, because in time of war their ships were
always in greater danger than those of the
British were. After the English Navy had
defeated the Spanish Armada in 1588 the
Spaniards began, slowly but surely, to lose
their chance of making a permanent Greater
Spain. After the great Dutch War, when
Blake defeated Van Tromp in 1653, there was
no further chance of a permanent Greater
Holland. And, even before the Dutch War and
the Armada, the Portuguese, who had once
ruled the Indian Ocean and who had conquered
Brazil, were themselves conquered by Spain
and shut out from all chance of establishing a
Greater Portugal.

So the one supreme point to be decided by
the Second Hundred Years' War lay between
only two rivals, France and Britain. Was
there to be a Greater France or a Greater
Britain across the seas ? The answer de-
pended on the rival navies. Of course, it
involved many other elements of national and
Imperial power on both sides. But no other
elements of power could have possibly pre-
vailed against a hostile and triumphant navy.

Everything that went to make a Greater France or a Greater Britain had to cross the sea—men, women, and children, horses and cattle, all the various appliances a civilized people must take with them when they settle in a new country. Every time there was war there were battles at sea, and these battles were nearly always won by the British. Every British victory at sea made it harder for French trade, because every ship between France and Greater France ran more risk of being taken, while every ship between Britain and Greater Britain stood a better chance of getting safely through. This affected everything on both competing sides in America. British business went on. French business almost stopped dead. Even the trade with the Indians living a thousand miles inland was changed in favour of the British and against the French, as all the guns and knives and beads and everything else that the white man offered to the Indian in exchange for his furs had to come across the sea, which was just like an enemy's country to every French ship, but just like her own to every British one. Thus the victors at sea grew continually stronger in America, while the losers grew correspondingly weaker. When peace came, the French only had time enough

to build new ships and start their trade again
before the next war set them back once
more ; while the British had nearly all their
old ships, all those they had taken from the
French, and many new ones.

But where did Wolfe come in ? He came in
at the most important time and place of all,
and he did the most important single deed
of all. This brings us to the consideration of
how the whole of the Second Hundred Years'
War was won, not by the British Navy alone,
much less by the Army alone, but by the united
service of both, fighting like the two arms of
one body, the Navy being the right arm and
the Army the left. The heart of this whole
Second Hundred Years' War was the Seven
Years' War ; the British part of the Seven
Years' War was then called the 'Maritime
War' ; and the heart of the 'Maritime War'
was the winning of Canada, in which the
decisive blow was dealt by Wolfe.

We shall see presently how Navy and Army
worked together as a united service in 'joint
expeditions' by sea and land, how Wolfe took
part in two other joint expeditions before he
commanded the land force of the one at
Quebec, and how the mighty empire-making
statesman, William Pitt, won the day for

Britain and for Greater Britain, with Lord Anson at the head of the Navy to help him, and Saunders in command at the front. It was thus that the age-long vexed question of a Greater France or a Greater Britain in America was finally decided by the sword. The conquering sword was that of the British Empire as a whole. But the hand that wielded it was Pitt; the hilt was Anson, the blade was Saunders, and the point was Wolfe.

CHAPTER V

LOUISBOURG

1758

IN 1755 Wolfe was already writing what he thought were farewell letters before going off to the war. And that very year the war, though not formally declared till the next, actually did break out in America, where a British army under Braddock, with Washington as his aide-de-camp, was beaten in Ohio by the French and Indians. Next year the French, owing to the failure of Admiral Byng and the British fleet to assist the garrison, were able to capture Minorca in the Mediterranean; while their new general in Canada, Montcalm, Wolfe's great opponent, took Oswego. The triumph of the French fleet at Minorca made the British people furious. Byng was court-martialled, found guilty of failure to do his utmost to save Minorca, and condemned to death. In spite of Pitt's efforts to save him, the sentence was carried out and he was shot

WILLIAM PITT, EARL OF CHATHAM

From the National Portrait Gallery

on the quarter-deck of his own flagship. Two other admirals, Hawke and Saunders, both of whom were soon to see service with Wolfe, were then sent out as a ' cargo of courage ' to retrieve the British position at sea. By this time preparations were being hurried forward on every hand. Fleets were fitting out. Armies were mustering. And, best of all, Pitt was just beginning to make his influence felt.

In 1757, the third year of war, things still went badly for the British at the front. In America Montcalm took Fort William Henry, and a British fleet and army failed to accomplish anything against Louisbourg. In Europe another British fleet and army were fitted out to go on another joint expedition, this time against Rochefort, a great seaport in the west of France. The senior staff officer, next to the three generals in command, was Wolfe, now thirty years of age. The admiral in charge of the fleet was Hawke, as famous a fighter as Wolfe himself. A little later, when both these great men were known throughout the whole United Service, as well as among the millions in Britain and in Greater Britain, their names were coupled in countless punning toasts, and patriots from Canada to Calcutta would stand up to drink a health to ' the eye of a Hawke

and the heart of a Wolfe.'   But Wolfe was not
a general yet; and the three pottering old
men who were generals at Rochefort could not
make up their minds to do anything but talk.
These generals had been ordered to take
Rochefort by complete surprise.   But after
spending five days in front of it, so that every
Frenchman could see what they had come for,
they decided to countermand the attack and
sail home.

Wolfe was a very angry and disgusted man.
Yet, though this joint expedition was a dis-
graceful failure, he had learned some useful
lessons, which he was presently to turn to good
account.   He saw, at least, what such expeditions should not attempt; and that a
general should act boldly, though wisely, with
the fleet.   More than this, he had himself
made a plan which his generals were too timid
to carry out; and this plan was so good that
Pitt, now in supreme control for the next four
years, made a note of it and marked him down
for promotion and command.

Both came sooner than any one could have
expected.   Pitt was sick of fleets and armies
that did nothing but hold councils of war and
then come back to say that the enemy could
not be safely attacked.   He made up his mind

to send out real fighters with the next joint expedition. So in 1758 he appointed Wolfe as the junior of the three brigadier-generals under Amherst, who was to join Admiral Boscawen—nicknamed ' Old Dreadnought '— in a great expedition meant to take Louisbourg for good and all.

Louisbourg was the greatest fortress in America. It was in the extreme east of Canada, on the island of Cape Breton, near the best fishing-grounds, and on the flank of the ship channel into the St Lawrence. A fortress there, in which French fleets could shelter safely, was like a shield for New France and a sword against New England. In 1745, just before the outbreak of the Jacobite rebellion in Scotland, an army of New Englanders under Sir William Pepperrell, with the assistance of Commodore Warren's fleet, had taken this fortress. But at the peace of Aix-la-Chapelle in 1748, when Wolfe had just come of age, it was given back to France.

Ten years later, when Wolfe went out to join the second army that was sent against it, the situation was extremely critical. Both French and British strained every nerve, the one to hold, the other to take, the greatest fortress in America. A French fleet sailed

from Brest in the spring and arrived safely.
But it was not nearly strong enough to
attempt a sea-fight off Louisbourg, and three
smaller fleets that were meant to join it were
all smashed up off the coast of France by the
British, who thus knew, before beginning the
siege, that Louisbourg could hardly expect any
help from outside. Hawke was one of the
British smashers this year. The next year
he smashed up a much greater force in
Quiberon Bay, and so made 'the eye of
a Hawke and the heart of a Wolfe' work
together again, though they were thousands
of miles apart and one directed a fleet while
the other inspired an army.

The fortress of Louisbourg was built beside
a fine harbour with an entrance still further
defended by a fortified island. It was garri-
soned by about four thousand four hundred
soldiers. Some of these were hired Germans,
who cared nothing for the French ; and the
French-Canadian and Indian irregulars were
not of much use at a regular siege. The British
admiral Boscawen had a large fleet, and General
Amherst an army twelve thousand strong.
Taking everything into account, by land and
sea, the British united service at the siege was
quite three times as strong as the French

united service. But the French ships, manned
by three thousand sailors, were in a good
harbour, and they and the soldiers were defended by thick walls with many guns. Besides, the whole defence was conducted by
Drucour, as gallant a leader as ever drew
sword.

Boscawen was chosen by Pitt for the same
reason as Wolfe had been, because he was a
fighter. He earned his nickname of ' Old
Dreadnought ' from the answer he made one
night in the English Channel when the officer
of the watch called him to say that two big
French ships were bearing down on his single
British one. ' What are we to do, sir ? '
asked the officer. ' Do ? ' shouted Boscawen,
springing out of his berth, ' Do ?—Why, damn
'em, fight 'em, of course ! ' And they did.
Amherst was the slow-and-sure kind of
general ; but he had the sense to know a good
man when he saw one, and to give Wolfe the
chance of trying his own quick-and-sure way
instead.

A portion of the British fleet under
Vice-Admiral Sir Charles Hardy had been
cruising off Louisbourg for some time before
Boscawen's squadron hove in sight on June 2.
This squadron was followed by more than

twice its own number of ships carrying the
army. All together, there were a hundred
and fifty-seven British vessels, besides Hardy's
covering squadron. Of course, the men could
not be landed under the fire of the fortress.
But two miles south of it, and running westward from it for many miles more, was Gabarus
Bay with an open beach. For several days the
Atlantic waves dashed against the shore so
furiously that no boat could live through
their breakers. But on the eighth the three
brigades of infantry made for three different
points,[1] respectively two, three, and four miles
from the fortress. The French sent out half
the garrison to shoot down the first boatloads
that came in on the rollers. To cover the landing, some of Boscawen's ships moved in as
close as they could and threw shells inshore :
but without dislodging the enemy.

Each of the three brigades had its own flag
—one red, another blue, and the third white.
Wolfe's brigade was the red, the one farthest
west from Louisbourg, and Wolfe's did the
fighting. While the boats rose and fell on the
gigantic rollers and the enemy's cannon roared
and the waves broke in thunder on the beach,

[1] White Point, Flat Point, and Kennington Cove. See the
accompanying Map of the siege.

VIEW OF LOUISBOURG IN 1758

From an engraving in the Dominion Archives

Wolfe was standing up in the stern-sheets, scanning every inch of the ground to see if there was no place where a few men could get a footing and keep it till the rest had landed. He had first-rate soldiers with him : grenadiers, Highlanders, and light infantry.

The boats were now close in, and the French were firing cannon and muskets into them right and left. One cannon-ball whizzed across Wolfe's own boat and smashed his flagstaff to splinters. Just then three young light infantry officers saw a high ledge of rocks, under shelter of which a few men could form up. Wolfe, directing every movement with his cane, like Gordon in China a century later, shouted to the others to follow them ; and then, amid the crash of artillery and the wild welter of the surf, though many boats were smashed and others upset, though some men were shot and others drowned, the landing was securely made. 'Who were the first ashore ?' asked Wolfe, as the men were forming up under the ledge. Two Highlanders were pointed out. 'Good fellows!' he said, as he went up to them and handed each a guinea.

While the ranks were forming on the beach, the French were firing into them and men were dropping fast. But every gap was closed as soon

as it was made. Directly Wolfe saw he had
enough men he sprang to the front; where-
upon they all charged after him, straight at
the batteries on the crest of the rising shore.
Here there was some wild work for a minute
or two, with swords, bayonets, and muskets all
hard at it. But the French now saw, to their
dismay, that thousands of other redcoats were
clambering ashore, nearer in to Louisbourg,
and that these men would cut them off if they
waited a moment longer. So they turned and
ran, hotly pursued, till they were safe in under
the guns of the fortress. A deluge of shot and
shell immediately belched forth against the
pursuing British, who wisely halted just out of
range.

After this exciting commencement Amherst's
guns, shot, shell, powder, stores, food, tents,
and a thousand other things had all to be
landed on the surf-lashed, open beach. It
was the sailors' stupendous task to haul the
whole of this cumbrous material up to the
camp. The bluejackets, however, were not
the only ones to take part in the work, for the
ships' women also turned to, with the best of a
gallant goodwill. In a few days all the material
was landed; and Amherst, having formed his
camp, sat down to conduct the siege.

Louisbourg harbour faces east, runs in westward nearly a mile, and is over two miles from north to south. The north and south points, however, on either side of its entrance, are only a mile apart. On the south point stood the fortress; on the north the lighthouse; and between were several islands, rocks, and bars that narrowed the entrance for ships to only three cables, or a little more than six hundred yards. Wolfe saw that the north point, where the lighthouse stood, was undefended, and might be seized and used as a British battery to smash up the French batteries on Goat Island at the harbour mouth. Acting on this idea, he marched with twelve hundred men across the stretch of country between the British camp and the lighthouse. The fleet brought round his guns and stores and all other necessaries by sea. A tremendous bombardment then silenced every French gun on Goat Island. This left the French nothing for their defence but the walls of Louisbourg itself.

Both French and British soon realized that the fall of Louisbourg was only a question of time. But time was everything to both. The British were anxious to take Louisbourg and then sail up to Quebec and take it by

a sudden attack while Montcalm was engaged in fighting Abercromby's army on Lake
Champlain. The French, of course, were
anxious to hold out long enough to prevent
this; and Drucour, their commandant at
Louisbourg, was just the man for their purpose.
His wife, too, was as brave as he. She used
to go round the batteries cheering up the
gunners, and paying no more attention to the
British shot and shell than if they had been
only fireworks. On June 18, just before
Wolfe's lighthouse batteries were ready to
open fire, Madame Drucour set sail in the
venturesome *Echo*, a little French man-
of-war that was making a dash for it, in
the hope of carrying the news to Quebec.
But after a gallant fight the *Echo* had to
haul down her colours to the *Juno* and the
Sutherland. We shall hear more of the
Sutherland at the supreme moment of Wolfe's
career.

Nothing French, not even a single man,
could now get into or out of Louisbourg. But
Drucour still kept the flag up, and sent out
parties at night to harass his assailants. One
of these surprised a British post, killed Lord
Dundonald who commanded it, and retired
safely after being almost cut off by British re-

inforcements. Though Wolfe had silenced the
island batteries and left the entrance open
enough for Boscawen to sail in, the admiral
hesitated because he thought he might lose
too many ships by risking it. Then the French
promptly sank some of their own ships at the
entrance to keep him out. But six hundred
British sailors rowed in at night and boarded
and took the only two ships remaining afloat.
The others had been blown up a month before
by British shells fired by naval gunners from
Amherst's batteries. Drucour was now in a
terrible plight. Not a ship was left. He was
completely cut off by land and sea. Many
of his garrison were dead, many more were
lying sick or wounded. His foreigners were
ready for desertion. His French Canadians
had grown down-hearted. All the non-com-
batants wished him to surrender at once.
What else could he do but give in ? On
July 27 he hauled down the fleurs-de-lis from
the great fortress. But he had gained his
secondary object ; for it was now much too
late in the year for the same British force to
begin a new campaign against Quebec.

Wolfe, like Nelson and Napoleon, was never
content to ' let well enough alone,' if anything better could possibly be done. When

the news came of Montcalm's great victory
over Abercromby at Ticonderoga, he told
Amherst he was ready to march inland at
once with reinforcements. And after Louisbourg had surrendered and Boscawen had
said it was too late to start for Quebec, he
again volunteered to do any further service
that Amherst required. The service he was
sent on was the soldier's most disgusting duty;
but he did it thoroughly, though he would
have preferred anything else. He went with
Hardy's squadron to destroy the French settlements along the Gulf of St Lawrence, so as to
cut off their supplies from the French in Quebec
before the next campaign.

After Rochefort Wolfe had become a marked
man. After Louisbourg he became an Imperial
hero. The only other the Army had yet pro-
duced in this war was Lord Howe, who had
been killed in a skirmish just before Ticonderoga. Wolfe knew Howe well, admired him
exceedingly, and called him 'the noblest
Englishman that has appeared in my time, and
the best soldier in the army.' He would have
served under him gladly. But Howe—young,
ardent, gallant, yet profound—was dead; and
the hopes of discerning judges were centred

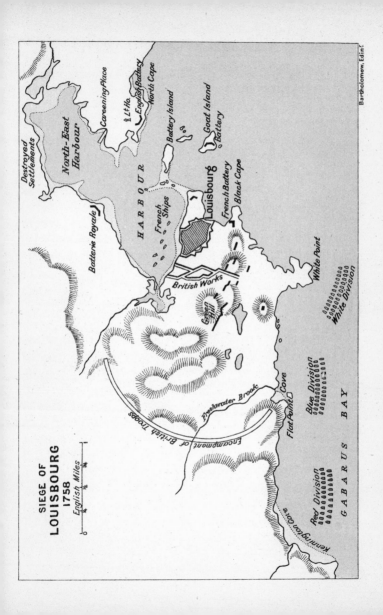

SIEGE OF
LOUISBOURG
1758
English Miles

Bartholomew, Edin.ʳ

Destroyed
Settlements

North-East
Harbour

Careening Place

Lt. Ho.

English Battery

North Cape

Batterie Royale

HARBOUR

French
Ships

Battery Island

Goat Island
Battery

Louisbourg

French Battery

Black Cape

British Works

White Point

Green Hill

White Division

Encampment of British Troops

Freshwater Brook

Kennington Cove

Blue Division

Flat Point   Cove

GABARUS   BAY

Red Division

on Wolfe. The war had not been going well, and this victory at Louisbourg was the first that the British people could really rejoice over with all their heart.

The British colonies went wild with delight. Halifax had a state ball, at which Wolfe danced to his heart's content; while his unofficial partners thought themselves the luckiest girls in all America to be asked by the hero of Louisbourg. Boston and Philadelphia had large bonfires and many fireworks. The chief people of New York attended a gala dinner. Every church had special thanksgivings.

In England the excitement was just as great, and Wolfe's name and fame flew from lip to lip all over the country. Parliament passed special votes of thanks. Medals were struck to celebrate the event. The king stood on his palace steps to receive the captured colours, which were carried through London in triumph by the Guards and the Household Brigade. And Pitt, the greatest—and, in a certain sense, the only—British statesman who has ever managed people, parliament, government, navy, and army, all together, in a world-wide Imperial war—Pitt, the eagle-eyed and lion-hearted, at once marked Wolfe

down again for higher promotion and, this
time, for the command of an army of his own.
And ever since the Empire Year of 1759 the
world has known that Pitt was right.

CHAPTER VI

QUEBEC

1759

In October 1758 Wolfe sailed from Halifax for England with Boscawen and very nearly saw a naval battle off Land's End with the French fleet returning to France from Quebec. The enemy, however, slipped away in the dark. On November 1 he landed at Portsmouth. He had been made full colonel of a new regiment, the 67th Foot (Hampshires), and before going home to London he set off to see it at Salisbury.[1] Wolfe's old regiment, the 20th (Lancashire Fusiliers), was now in Germany, fighting under the command of Prince Ferdinand of Brunswick, and was soon to win more laurels at Minden, the first of the three great British

[1] Ten years later a Russian general saw this regiment at Minorca and was loud in his praise of its all-round excellence, when Wolfe's successor in the colonelcy, Sir James Campbell, at once said : ' The only merit due to me is the strictness with which I have followed the system introduced by the hero of Quebec.'

victories of 1759 — Minden, Quebec, and Quiberon.

Though far from well, Wolfe was as keen as ever about anything that could possibly make him fit for command. He picked out the best officers with a sure eye: generals and colonels, like Carleton; captains, like Delaune, a man made for the campaigns in Canada, who, as we shall see later, led the 'Forlorn Hope' up the Heights of Abraham. Wolfe had also noted in a third member of the great Howe family a born leader of light infantry for Quebec. Wolfe was very strong on light infantry, and trained them to make sudden dashes with a very short but sharp surprise attack followed by a quick retreat under cover. One day at Louisbourg an officer said this reminded him of what Xenophon wrote about the Carduchians who harassed the rear of the world-famous 'Ten Thousand.' 'I had it from Xenophon' was Wolfe's reply. Like all great commanders, Wolfe knew what other great commanders had done and thought, no matter to what age or nation they belonged: Greek, Roman, German, French, British, or any other. Years before this he had recommended a young officer to study the Prussian Army Regulations and Vauban's book on

Sieges. Nor did he forget to read the lives of men like Scanderbeg and Ziska, who could teach him many unusual lessons. He kept his eyes open everywhere, all his life long, on men and things and books. He recommended his friend, Captain Rickson, who was then in Halifax, to read Montesquieu's not yet famous book *The Spirit of Laws*, because it would be useful for a government official in a new country. Writing home to his mother from Louisbourg about this new country, that is, before Canada had become British, before there was much more than a single million of English-speaking people in the whole New World, and before most people on either side of the Atlantic understood what a great over-sea empire meant at all, he said: 'This will, sometime hence, be a vast empire, the seat of power and learning. Nature has refused them nothing, and there will grow a people out of our little spot, England, that will fill this vast space, and divide this great portion of the globe with the Spaniards, who are possessed of the other half of it.'

On arriving in England Wolfe had reported his presence to the commander-in-chief, Lord Ligonier, requesting leave of absence in order that he might visit his relatives. This was granted, and the Wolfe family met together once more and for the last time.

Though he said little about it, Wolfe must have snatched some time for Katherine Lowther, his second love, to whom he was now engaged. What had happened between him and his first love, Miss Lawson, will probably never be known. We know that his parents were opposed to his marrying her. Perhaps, too, she may not have been as much in love as he was. But, for whatever reason, they parted. Then he fell in love with beautiful Katherine Lowther, a sister to the Earl of Lonsdale and afterwards Duchess of Bolton.

Meanwhile Pitt was planning for his Empire Year of 1759, the year of Ferdinand at Minden, Wolfe at Quebec, and Hawke in Quiberon Bay. Before Pitt had taken the war in hand nearly everything had gone against the British. Though Clive had become the British hero of India in 1757, and Wolfe of Louisbourg in 1758, there had hitherto been more defeats than victories. Minorca had been lost in 1756; in America Braddock's army had been destroyed in 1755; and Montcalm had won victories at Oswego in 1756, at Fort William Henry in 1757, and at Ticonderoga in

1758. More than this, in 1759 the French were preparing fleets and armies to invade England, Ireland, and Scotland; and the British people were thinking rather of their own defence at home than of attacking the French abroad.

Pitt, however, rightly thought that vigorous attacks from the sea were the best means of defence at home. From London he looked out over the whole world : at France and her allies in the centre, at French India on his far left, and at French Canada on his far right; with the sea dividing his enemies and uniting his friends, if only he could hold its highways with the British Navy.

To carry out his plans Pitt sent a small army and a great deal of money to Frederick the Great, to help him in the middle of Europe against the Russians, Austrians, and French. At the same time he let Anson station fleets round the coast of France, so that no strong French force could get at Britain or Greater Britain, or go to help Greater France, without a fight at sea. Then, having cut off Canada from France and taken her outpost at Louisbourg, he aimed a death-blow at her very heart by sending Saunders, with a quarter of the whole British Navy, against Quebec, the stronghold of New France, where the land attack was to be made by a little army of 9000 men under Wolfe. Even this was not the whole of Pitt's plan for the conquest of Canada. A smaller army was to be sent against the French on the Great Lakes, and a larger one, under Amherst, along the line of Lake Champlain, towards Montreal.

Pitt did a very bold thing when he took a young colonel and asked the king to make him a general and allow him to choose his own brigadiers and staff officers. It was a bold thing, because, whenever there is a position of honour to be given, the older men do not like being passed over and all the politicians who think of themselves first and their country afterwards wish to put in their own favourites. Wolfe, of course, had enemies. Dullards often think that men of genius are crazy, and some one had told the king that Wolfe was mad. ' Mad, is he ? ' said the king, remembering all the recent British defeats on land; ' then I hope he 'll bite some of my other generals ! ' Wolfe was not able to give any of his seniors his own and Lord Howe's kind of divine ' madness ' during that war. But he did give a touch of it to many of his juniors; with the result that his Quebec army was better officered

than any other British land force of the
time.

The three brigadiers next in command to
Wolfe—Monckton, Townshend, and Murray—
were not chosen simply because they were all
sons of peers, but because, like Howe and
Boscawen, they were first-rate officers as well.
Barré and Carleton were the two chief men on
the staff. Each became celebrated in later
days, Barré in parliament, and Carleton as
both the saviour of Canada from the American
attack in 1775 and the first British governor-
general. Williamson, the best gunnery expert
in the whole Army, commanded the artillery.
The only troublesome officer was Townshend,
who thought himself, and whose family and
political friends thought him, at least as good
a general as Wolfe, if not a better one. But
even Townshend did his duty well. The army
at Halifax was supposed to be twelve thousand,
but its real strength was only nine thousand.
The difference was mostly due to the ravages
of scurvy and camp fever, both of which, in
their turn, were due to the bad food supplied
by rascally contractors. The action of the
officers alone saved the situation from becoming
desperate. Indeed, if it had not been for what
the officers did for their men in the way of

buying better food, at great cost, out of their own not well-filled pockets, there might have been no army at all to greet Wolfe on his arrival in America.

The fleet was the greatest that had ever sailed across the seas. It included one-quarter of the whole Royal Navy. There were 49 men-of-war manned by 14,000 sailors and marines. There were also more than 200 vessels—transports, store ships, provision ships, etc.—manned by about 7000 merchant seamen. Thus there were at least twice as many sailors as soldiers at the taking of Quebec. Saunders was a most capable admiral. He had been flag-lieutenant during Anson's famous voyage round the world; then Hawke's best fighting captain during the war in which Wolfe was learning his work at Dettingen and Laffeldt; and then Hawke's second-in-command of the ' cargo of courage ' sent out after Byng's disgrace at Minorca. After Quebec he crowned his fine career by being one of the best first lords of the Admiralty that ever ruled the Navy. Durell, his next in command, was slower than Amherst; and Amherst never made a short cut in his life, even to certain success. Holmes, the third admiral, was thoroughly efficient. Hood, a still better

admiral than any of those at Quebec, afterwards served under Holmes, and Nelson under
Hood ; which links Trafalgar with Quebec.
But a still closer link with ' mighty Nelson '
was Jervis, who took charge of Wolfe's personal
belongings at Quebec the night before the
battle and many years later became Nelson's
commander-in-chief. Another Quebec captain
who afterwards became a great admiral was
Hughes, famous for his fights in India. But
the man whose subsequent fame in the world
at large eclipsed that of any other in this fleet
was Captain Cook, who made the first good
charts of Canadian waters some years before
he became a great explorer in the far Pacific.

There was a busy scene at Portsmouth on
February 17, when Saunders and Wolfe sailed
in the flagship H.M.S. *Neptune*, of 90 guns and
a crew of 750 men. She was one of the well-
known old ' three-deckers,' those ' wooden
walls of England ' that kept the Empire safe
while it was growing up. The guard of red-
coated marines presented arms, and the
hundreds of bluejackets were all in their places
as the two commanders stepped on board.
The naval officers on the quarter-deck were
very spick and span in their black three-
cornered hats, white wigs, long, bright blue,

gold-laced coats, white waistcoats and breeches and stockings, and gold-buckled shoes. The idea of having naval uniforms of blue and white and gold—the same colours that are worn to-day—came from the king's seeing the pretty Duchess of Bedford in a blue-and-white riding-habit, which so charmed him that he swore he would make the officers wear the same colours for the uniforms just then being newly tried. This was when the Duke of Bedford was first lord of the Admiralty, some years before Pitt's great expedition against Quebec.

The sailors were also in blue and white; but they were not so spick and span as the officers. They were a very rough-and-ready-looking lot. They wore small, soft, three-cornered black hats, bright blue jackets, open enough to show their coarse white shirts, and coarse white duck trousers. They had shoes without stockings on shore, and only bare feet on board. They carried cutlasses and pistols, and wore their hair in pigtails. They would be a surprising sight to modern eyes. But not so much so as the women! Ships and regiments in those days always had a certain number of women for washing and mending the clothes. There

was one woman to about every twenty men.
They drew pay and were under regular orders,
just like the soldiers and sailors. Sometimes
they gave a willing hand in action, helping the
' powder-monkeys '—boys who had to pass
the powder from the barrels to the gunners—
or even taking part in a siege, as at Louisbourg.

The voyage to Halifax was long, rough,
and cold, and Wolfe was sea-sick as ever.
Strangely enough, these ships coming out to
the conquest of Canada under St George's cross
made land on St George's Day near the place
where Cabot had raised St George's cross over
Canadian soil before Columbus had set foot
on the mainland of America. But though
April 23 might be a day of good omen, it was
a very bleak one that year off Cape Breton,
where ice was packed for miles and miles
along the coast. On the 30th the fleet entered
Halifax. Slow old Durell was hurried off on
May 5 with eight men-of-war and seven
hundred soldiers under Carleton to try to stop
any French ships from getting up to Quebec.
Carleton was to go ashore at Isle-aux-Coudres,
an island commanding the channel sixty miles
below Quebec, and mark out a passage for the
fleet through the ' Traverse ' at the lower end
of the island of Orleans, thirty miles higher up.

On the 13th Saunders sailed for Louisbourg,
where the whole expedition was to meet and
get ready. Here Wolfe spent the rest of May,
working every day and all day. His army,
with the exception of nine hundred American
rangers, consisted of seasoned British regulars,
with all the weaklings left behind ; and it
did his heart good to see them on parade.
There was the 15th, whose officers still wear a
line of black braid on their uniforms in mourning for his death. The 15th and five other
regiments—the 28th, 43rd, 47th, 48th, and
58th—were English. But the 35th had been
forty years in Ireland, and was Irish to a man.
The whole seven regiments were dressed very
much alike : three-cornered, stiff black hats
with black cockades, white wigs, long-tailed
red coats turned back with blue or white in
front, where they were fastened only at the
neck, white breeches, and long white gaiters
coming over the knee. A very different corps
was the 78th, or ' Fraser's,' Highlanders, one
of the regiments Wolfe first recommended and
Pitt first raised. Only fourteen years before
the Quebec campaign these same Highlanders had joined Prince Charlie, the Young
Pretender, in the famous ' '45.' They were
mostly Roman Catholics, which accounts for

the way they intermarried with the French
Canadians after the conquest. They had been
fighting for the Stuarts against King George,
and Wolfe, as we have seen, had himself fought
against them at Culloden. Yet here they were
now, under Wolfe, serving King George. They
knew that the Stuart cause was lost for ever;
and all of them, chiefs and followers alike,
loved the noble profession of arms. The
Highlanders then wore 'bonnets' like a high
tam-o'-shanter, with one white curly feather
on the left side. Their red coats were faced
with yellow, and they wore the Fraser plaid
hung from the shoulders and caught up,
loopwise, on both hips. Their kilts were very
short and not pleated. Badger sporrans, show-
ing the head in the middle, red-and-white-
diced hose, and buckled brogues completed
their wild but martial dress, which was well
set off by the dirks and claymores that swung
to the stride of the mountaineer.

Each regiment had one company of grenadiers, picked out for their size, strength, and
steadiness, and one company of light infantry,
picked out for their quickness and good marks-
manship. Sometimes all the grenadier companies would be put together in a separate
battalion. The same thing was often done

with the light infantry companies, which were then led by Colonel Howe. Wolfe had also made up a small three-company battalion of picked grenadiers from the five regiments that were being left behind at Louisbourg to guard the Maritime Provinces. This little battalion became famous at Quebec as the ' Louisbourg Grenadiers.' The grenadiers all wore red and white, like the rest, except that their coats were buttoned up the whole way, and instead of the three-cornered hats they wore high ones like a bishop's mitre. The artillery wore blue-grey coats turned back with red, yellow braid, and half-moon-shaped black hats, with the points down towards their shoulders.

The only remaining regiment is of much greater interest in connection with a Canadian campaign. It was the 60th Foot, then called the Royal Americans, afterwards the Sixtieth Rifles or ' Old Sixtieth,' and now the King's Royal Rifle Corps. It was the first regiment of regulars ever raised in Greater Britain, and the first to introduce the rifle-green uniform now known all over the Empire, especially in Canada, where all rifle regiments still follow ' the 60th's ' lead so far as that is possible. Many of its officers and men who returned from the conquest of Canada to their homes in the British colonies were destined to move on to Canada with their families as United Empire Loyalists. This was their first war ; and they did so well in it that Wolfe gave them the rifle-man's motto they still bear in token of their smartness and dash—*Celer et Audax*. Un-fortunately they did not then wear the famous ' rifle green ' but the ordinary red. Un-fortunately, too, the rifleman's green has no connection with the ' green jackets of American backwoodsmen in the middle of the eighteenth century.' The backwoodsmen were not dressed in green as a rule, and they never formed any considerable part of the regiment at any time. The first green uniform came in with the new 5th battalion in 1797 ; and the old 2nd and 3rd battalions, which fought under Wolfe, did not adopt it till 1815. It was not even of British origin, but an imitation of a German hussar uniform which was itself an imitation of one worn by the Hungarians, who have the senior hussars of the world. But though Wolfe's Royal Americans did not wear the rifle green, and though their coats and waistcoats were of common red, their uni-forms differed from those of all other regi-ments at Quebec in several particulars. The most remarkable difference was the absence of lace, an absence specially authorized only for this corps, and then only in view of special service and many bush fights in America. The double-breasted coats were made to button across, except at the top, where the lapels turned back, like the cuffs and coat-tails. All these 'turnbacks' and the breeches were blue. The very long gaiters, the waist and cross belts, the neckerchief and hat piping were white. Wearing this distinctively plain uniform, and led by their buglers and drummers in scarlet and gold, like state trumpeters, the Royal Americans could not, even at a distance, be mistaken for any other regiment.

On June 6 Saunders and Wolfe sailed for Quebec with a hundred and forty-one ships. Wolfe's work in getting his army safely off being over, he sat down alone in his cabin to make his will. His first thought was for Katherine Lowther, his *fiancée*, who was to have her own miniature portrait, which he carried with him, set in jewels and given back to her. Warde, Howe, and Carleton were each remembered. He left all the residue of his estate to ' my good mother,' his father having just died. More than a third of the whole will was taken up with providing for his servants. No wonder he was called 'the soldier's friend.'

There was a thrilling scene at Louisbourg as regiment after regiment marched down to the shore, with drums beating, bugles sounding, and colours flying. Each night, after drinking the king's health, they had drunk another toast—'British colours on every French fort, port, and garrison in North America.' Now here they were, the pick of the Army and Navy, off with Wolfe to raise those colours over Quebec, the most important military point on the whole continent. On they sailed, all together, till they reached the Saguenay, a hundred and twenty miles below Quebec. Here, on the afternoon of June 20, the sun shone down on a sight such as the New World had never seen before, and has never seen again. The river narrows opposite the Saguenay and is full of shoals and islands; so this was the last day the whole one hundred and forty-one vessels sailed together, in their three divisions, under those three ensigns—'The Red, White, and Blue '— which have made the British Navy loved, feared, and famous round the seven seas. What a sight it was! Thousands and thousands of soldiers and sailors crowded those

scores and scores of high-decked ships ; while
hundreds and hundreds of swelling sails
gleamed white against the sun, across the
twenty miles of blue St Lawrence.

Wolfe, however, was not there to see it.   He
had gone forward the day before.   A dispatch-
boat had come down from Durell to say that,
in spite of his advanced squadron, Bougainville, Montcalm's ablest brigadier, had slipped
through with twenty-three ships from France,
bringing out a few men and a good deal of
ammunition, stores, and food.   This gave
Quebec some sorely needed help.   Besides,
Montcalm had found out Pitt's plan ; and
nobody knew where the only free French
fleet was now.   It had wintered in the West
Indies.   But had it sailed for France or the
St Lawrence ?   At the first streak of dawn on
the 23rd Durell's look-out off Isle-aux-Coudres
reported many ships coming up the river under
a press of sail.   Could the French West Indian
fleet have slipped in ahead of Saunders, as
Bougainville had slipped in ahead of Durell
himself ?   There was a tense moment on
board of Durell's squadron and in Carleton's
camp, in the pale, grey light of early morning,
as the bugles sounded, the boatswains blew
their whistles and roared their orders, and all

hands came tumbling up from below and ran
to battle quarters with a rush of swift bare feet.
But the incoming vanship made the private
British signal, and both sides knew that all was
well.

For a whole week the great fleet of one hundred
and forty-one ships worked their way through
the narrow channel between Isle-aux-Coudres
and the north shore, and then dared the dangers
of the Traverse, below the island of Orleans,
where the French had never passed more than
one ship at a time, and that only with the
greatest caution. The British went through
quite easily, without a single accident. In two
days the great Captain Cook had sounded and
marked out the channel better than the French
had in a hundred and fifty years; and so
thoroughly was his work done that the British
officers could handle their vessels in these
French waters better without than with the
French pilots. Old Captain Killick took the
Goodwill through himself, just next ahead of
the *Richmond*, on board of which was Wolfe.
The captured French pilot in the *Goodwill* was
sure she would be lost if she did not go slow
and take more care. But Killick laughed at
him and said : ' Damn me, but I 'll convince
you an Englishman can go where a French-

man daren't show his nose! ' And he did.

On June 26 Wolfe arrived at the west end of the island of Orleans, in full view of Quebec. The twenty days' voyage from Louisbourg had ended and the twelve weeks' siege had begun.

At this point we must take the map and never put it aside till the final battle is over. A whole book could not possibly make Wolfe's work plain to any one without the map. But with the map we can easily follow every move in this, the greatest crisis in both Wolfe's career and Canada's history.

What Wolfe saw and found out was enough to daunt any general. He had a very good army, but it was small. He could count upon the help of a mighty fleet, but even British fleets cannot climb hills or make an enemy come down and fight. Montcalm, however, was weakened by many things. The governor, Vaudreuil, was a vain, fussy, and spiteful fool, with power enough to thwart Montcalm at every turn. The intendant, Bigot, was the greatest knave ever seen in Canada, and the head of a gang of official thieves who robbed the country and the wretched French Canadians right and left. The French army, all together, numbered nearly seventeen thousand, almost twice Wolfe's own; but the bulk of it was militia, half starved and badly armed. Both Vaudreuil and Bigot could and did interfere disastrously with the five different forces that should have been made into one army under Montcalm alone—the French regulars, the Canadian regulars, the Canadian militia, the French sailors ashore, and the Indians. Montcalm had one great advantage over Wolfe. He was not expected to fight or manœuvre in the open field. His duty was not to drive Wolfe away, or even to keep Amherst out of Canada. All he had to do was to hold Quebec throughout the summer. The autumn would force the British fleet to leave for ice-free waters. Then, if Quebec could only be held, a change in the fortunes of war, or a treaty of peace, might still keep Canada in French hands. Wolfe had either to tempt Montcalm out of Quebec or get into it himself; and he soon realized that he would have to do this with the help of Saunders alone; for Amherst in the south was crawling forward towards Montreal so slowly that no aid from him could be expected.

Montcalm's position certainly looked secure for the summer. His left flank was guarded by the Montmorency, a swift river that could be forded only by a few men at a time in a narrow place, some miles up, where the dense bush would give every chance to his Indians and Canadians. His centre was guarded by entrenchments running from the Montmorency to the St Charles, six miles of ground, rising higher and higher towards Montmorency, all of it defended by the best troops and the bulk of the army, and none of it having an inch of cover for an enemy in front. The mouth of the St Charles was blocked by booms and batteries. Quebec is a natural fortress; and above Quebec the high, steep cliffs stretched for miles and miles. These cliffs could be climbed by a few men in several places; but nowhere by a whole army, if any defenders were there in force; and the British fleet could not land an army without being seen soon enough to draw plenty of defenders to the same spot. Forty miles above Quebec the St Lawrence channel narrows to only a quarter of a mile, and the down current becomes very swift indeed. Above this channel was the small French fleet, which could stop a much larger one trying to get up, or could even block most of the fairway by sinking some of its own ships. Besides all these defences of man and nature the French had floating batteries

along the north shore. They also held the
Levis Heights on the south shore, opposite
Quebec, so that ships crowded with helpless
infantry could not, without terrible risk, run
through the intervening narrows, barely a
thousand yards wide.

A gale blowing down-stream was the first
trouble for the British fleet. Many of the
transports broke loose and a good deal of
damage was done to small vessels and boats.
Next night a greater danger threatened, when
the ebb-tide, running five miles an hour,
brought down seven French fireships, which
suddenly burst into flame as they rounded the
Point of Levy. There was a display of devil's
fireworks such as few men have ever seen or
could imagine. Sizzling, crackling, and roaring, the blinding flames leaped into the jet-
black sky, lighting up the camps of both
armies, where thousands of soldiers watched
these engines of death sweep down on the
fleet. Each of the seven ships was full of
mines, blowing up and hurling shot and shell
in all directions. The crowded mass of British
vessels seemed doomed to destruction. But
the first spurt of fire had hardly been noticed
before the men in the guard boats began to
row to the rescue. Swinging the grappling-

hooks round at arm's length, as if they were heaving the lead, the bluejackets made the fireships fast, the officers shouted, 'Give way!' and presently the whole infernal flotilla was safely stranded. But it was a close thing and very hot work, as one of the happy-go-lucky Jack tars said with more force than grace, when he called out to the boat beside him: 'Hullo, mate! Did you ever take hell in tow before?'

Vaudreuil now made Montcalm, who was under his orders, withdraw the men from the Levis Heights, and thus abandon the whole of the south shore in front of Quebec. Wolfe, delighted, at once occupied the same place, with half his army and most of his guns. Then he seized the far side of the Montmorency and made his main camp there, without, however, removing his hospitals and stores from his camp on the island of Orleans. So he now had three camps, not divided, but joined together, by the St Lawrence, where the fleet could move about between them in spite of anything the French could do. He then marched up the Montmorency to the fords, to try the French strength there, and to find out if he could cross the river, march down the open ground behind Montcalm, and attack him

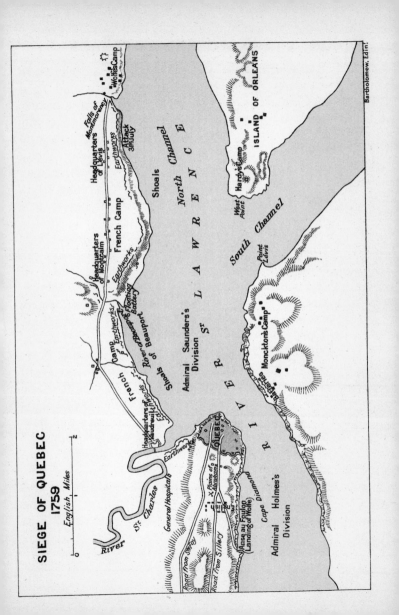

SIEGE OF QUEBEC
1759

English Miles

2
1
0

Wolfe's Camp

ISLAND OF ORLEANS

Hardy's Camp

West Point

Falls of Montmorency

Attack 31 July

Headquarters of Levis

Earthworks

Shoals

NORTH CHANNEL

French Camp

South CHANNEL

Point Levis

Headquarters of Montcalm

Earthworks

ST LAWRENCE

French Camp

Earthworks

River Beauport Floating Battery

Shoals of Beauport

Admiral Saunders's Division

Monckton's Camp

River St Charles

French Camp

Earthworks

Headquarters of Vaudreuil

RIVER

QUEBEC

Earthworks

General Hospital

X Plains of Abraham

Road from Sillery

Road from Sillery

Anse au Foulon (Landing of Wolfe)

Cape Diamond

Admiral Holmes's Division

Bartholomew, Edin.

from the rear. But he was repulsed at the first attempt, and saw that he could do no better at a second. Meanwhile his Levis batteries began a bombardment which lasted two months and reduced Quebec to ruins.

Yet he seemed as far off as ever from capturing the city. Battering down the houses of Quebec brought him no nearer to his object, while Montcalm's main body still stood securely in its entrenchments down at Beauport. Wolfe now felt he must try something decisive, even if desperate; and he planned an attack by land and water on the French left. Both French and British were hard at work on July 31. In the morning Wolfe sent one regiment marching up the Montmorency, as if to try the fords again, and another, also in full view of the French, up along the St Lawrence from the Levis batteries, as if it was to be taken over by the ships to the north shore above Quebec. Meanwhile Monckton's brigade was starting from the Point of Levy in row-boats, the *Centurion* was sailing down to the mouth of the Montmorency, two armed transports were being purposely run ashore on the beach at the top of the tide, and the *Pembroke, Trent, Lowestoff,* and *Racehorse* were taking up positions to cover the boats. The men-of-

war and Wolfe's batteries at Montmorency
then opened fire on the point he wished to
attack ; and both of them kept it up for eight
hours, from ten till six. All this time the
Levis batteries were doing their utmost against
Quebec. But Montcalm was not to be deceived. He saw that Wolfe intended to storm
the entrenchments at the point at which the
cannon were firing, and he kept the best of his
army ready to defend it.

Wolfe and the Louisbourg Grenadiers were
in the two armed transports when they
grounded at ten o'clock. To his disgust and to
Captain Cook's surprise both vessels stuck fast
in the mud nearly half a mile from shore.
This made the grenadiers' muskets useless
against the advanced French redoubt, which
stood at high-water mark, and which over-
matched the transports, because both of these
had grounded in such a way that they could
not bring their guns to bear in reply. The
stranded vessels soon became a death-trap.
Wolfe's cane was knocked out of his hand by
a cannon ball. Shells were bursting over the
deck, smashing the masts to pieces and sending splinters of wood and iron flying about
among the helpless grenadiers and gunners.
There was nothing to do but order the men

back to the boats and wait. The tide was not low till four. The weather was scorchingly hot. A thunderstorm was brewing. The redoubt could not be taken. The transports were a failure. And every move had to be made in full view of the watchful Montcalm, whose entrenchments at this point were on the top of a grassy hill nearly two hundred feet above the muddy beach.

But Wolfe still thought he might succeed with the main attack at low tide, although he had not been able to prepare it at high tide. His Montmorency batteries seemed to be pitching their shells very thickly into the French, and his three brigades of infantry were all ready to act together at the right time. Accordingly, for the hottest hours of that scorching day, Monckton's men grilled in the boats while Townshend's and Murray's waited in camp. At four the tide was low and Wolfe ordered the landing to begin.

The tidal flats ran out much farther than any one had supposed. The heavily laden boats stuck on an outer ledge and had to be cleared, shoved off, refilled with soldiers, and brought round to another place. It was now nearly six o'clock; and both sides were eager

for the fray. Townshend's and Murray's
brigades had forded the mouth of the Montmorency and were marching along to support
the attack, when, suddenly and unexpectedly,
the grenadiers spoiled it all ! Wolfe had ordered
the Louisbourg Grenadiers and the ten other
grenadier companies of the army to form up
and rush the redoubt. But, what with the
cheering of the sailors as they landed the rest
of Monckton's men, and their own eagerness
to come to close quarters at once, the Louisbourg men suddenly lost their heads and
charged before everything was ready. The rest
followed them pell-mell ; and in less than five
minutes the redoubt was swarming with excited
grenadiers, while the French who had held it
were clambering up the grassy hill into the
safer entrenchments.

The redoubt was certainly no place to stay
in. It had no shelter towards its rear ; and
dozens of French cannon and thousands of
French muskets were firing into it from the
heights. An immediate retirement was the
only proper course. But there was no holding
the men now. They broke into another mad
charge, straight at the hill. As they reached
it, amid a storm of musket balls and grape-
shot, the heavens joined in with a terrific storm

of their own. The rain burst in a perfect deluge; and the hill became almost impossible to climb, even if there had been no enemy pouring death-showers of fire from the top. When Wolfe saw what was happening he immediately sent officers running after the grenadiers to make them come back from the redoubt, and these officers now passed the word to retire at once. This time the grenadiers, all that were left of them, obeyed. Their two mad rushes had not lasted a quarter of an hour. Yet nearly half of the thousand men they started with were lying dead or wounded on that fatal ground.

Wolfe now saw that he was hopelessly beaten and that there was not a minute to lose in getting away. The boats could take only Monckton's men; and the rising tide would soon cut off Townshend's and Murray's from their camp beyond the mouth of the Montmorency. The two stranded transports, from which he had hoped so much that morning, were set on fire; and, under cover of their smoke and of the curtain of torrential rain, Monckton's crestfallen men got into their boats once more. Townshend's and Murray's brigades, enraged at not being brought into action, turned to march back by the way they had come so eagerly only an hour before. They moved off in perfect order; but, as they left the battlefield, they waved their hats in defiance at the jeering Frenchmen, challenging them to come down and fight it out with bayonets hand to hand.

Many gallant deeds were done that afternoon; but none more gallant than those of Captain Ochterloney and Lieutenant Peyton, both grenadier officers in the Royal Americans. Ochterloney had just been wounded in a duel; but he said his country's honour came before his own, and, sick and wounded as he was, he spent those panting hours in the boats without a murmur and did all he could to form his men up under fire. In the second charge he fell, shot through the lungs, with Peyton beside him, shot through the leg. When Wolfe called the grenadiers back a rescue party wanted to carry off both officers, to save them from the scalping-knife. But Ochterloney said he would never leave the field after such a defeat; and Peyton said he would never leave his captain. Presently a Canadian regular came up with two Indians, grabbed Ochterloney's watch, sword and money, and left the Indians to finish him. One of these savages clubbed him with a musket, while the other shot him in the chest and dashed in with a scalping-knife. In the meantime, Peyton crawled on his hands and knees to a double-barrelled musket and shot one Indian dead, but missed the other. This savage now left Ochterloney, picked up a bayonet and rushed at Peyton, who drew his dagger. A terrible life-and-death fight followed; but Peyton at last got a good point well driven home, straight through the Indian's heart. A whole scalping party now appeared. Ochterloney was apparently dead, and Peyton was too exhausted to fight any more. But, at this very moment, another British party came back for the rest of the wounded and carried Peyton off to the boats.

Then the Indians came back to scalp Ochterloney. By this time, however, some French regulars had come down, and one of them, finding Ochterloney still alive, drove off the Indians at the point of the bayonet, secured help, and carried him up the hill. Montcalm had him carefully taken into the General Hospital, where he was tenderly nursed by the nuns. Two days after he had been rescued, a French officer came out for his clothes and other effects. Wolfe then sent in twenty guineas for his rescuer, with a promise that, in return for the kindness shown to Ochterloney, the General Hospital would be specially protected if the British took Quebec. Towards the end of August Ochterloney died ; and both sides ceased firing while a French captain came out to report his death and return his effects.

This was by no means the only time the two enemies treated each other like friends. A party of French ladies were among the prisoners brought in to Wolfe one day ; and they certainly had no cause to complain of him. He gave them a dinner, at which he charmed them all by telling them about his visit to Paris. The next morning he sent them into Quebec with his aide-de-camp under a flag of truce. Another time the French officers sent him a kind of wine which was not to be had in the British camp, and he sent them some not to be had in their own.

But the stern work of war went on and on, though the weary month of August did not seem to bring victory any closer than disastrous July. Wolfe knew that September was to be the end of the campaign, the now-or-never of his whole career. And, knowing this, he set to work—head and heart and soul—on making the plan that brought him victory, death, and everlasting fame.

CHAPTER VII

THE PLAINS OF ABRAHAM

September 13, 1759

ON August 19 an aide-de-camp came out of
the farmhouse at Montmorency which served
as the headquarters of the British army to say
that Wolfe was too ill to rise from his bed.
The bad news spread like wildfire through
the camp and fleet, and soon became known
among the French. A week passed; but
Wolfe was no better. Tossing about on his
bed in a fever, he thought bitterly of his double
defeat, of the critical month of September,
of the grim strength of Quebec, formed by
nature for a stronghold, and then—worse still
—of his own weak body, which made him
most helpless just when he should have been
most fit for his duty.

Feeling that he could no longer lead in
person, he dictated a letter to the brigadiers,
sent them the secret instructions he had received from Pitt and the king, and asked them

to think over his three new plans for attacking
Montcalm at Beauport. They wrote back to
say they thought the defeats at the upper
fords of the Montmorency and at the heights
facing the St Lawrence showed that the
French could not be beaten by attacking the
Beauport lines again, no matter from what
side the attack was made. They then gave
him a plan of their own, which was, to convey
the army up the St Lawrence and fight their
way ashore somewhere between Cap Rouge,
nine miles above Quebec, and Pointe-aux-
Trembles, twenty-two miles above. They argued
that, by making a landing there, the British
could cut off Montcalm's communications with
Three Rivers and Montreal, from which his army
drew its supplies. Wolfe's letter was dictated
from his bed of sickness on the 26th. The
brigadiers answered him on the 29th. Saunders
talked it all over with him on the 31st.
Before this the fate of Canada had been an
affair of weeks. Now it was a matter of
days ; for the morrow would dawn on the
very last possible month of the siege—
September.

After his talk with Saunders Wolfe wrote
his last letter home to his mother, telling her
of his desperate plight :

The enemy puts nothing to risk, and I can't in conscience put the whole army to risk. My antagonist has wisely shut himself up in inaccessible entrenchments, so that I can't get at him without spilling a torrent of blood, and that perhaps to little purpose. The Marquis de Montcalm is at the head of a great number of bad soldiers and I am at the head of a small number of good ones, that wish for nothing so much as to fight him ; but the wary old fellow avoids an action, doubtful of the behaviour of his army. People must be of the profession to understand the disadvantages and difficulties we labour under, arising from the uncommon natural strength of the country.

On September 2 he wrote his last letter to Pitt. He had asked the doctors to 'patch him up,' saying that if they could make him fit for duty for only the next few days they need not trouble about what might happen to him afterwards. Their 'patching up' certainly cleared his fevered brain, for this letter was a masterly account of the whole siege and the plans just laid to bring it to an end. The style was so good, indeed, that Charles Townshend said his brother George must have been the real author, and that Wolfe, whom he dubbed ' a fiery-headed fellow, only fit for fighting,' could not have done any more than sign his name. But when George Townshend's own official letter about the battle in which Wolfe fell was also published, and was found to be much less effective than Wolfe's, Selwyn went up to Charles Townshend and said : ' Look here, Charles, if your brother wrote Wolfe's letter, who the devil wrote your brother's ? '

Wolfe did not try to hide anything from Pitt. He told him plainly about the two defeats and the terrible difficulties in the way of winning any victory. The whole letter is too long for quotation, and odd scraps from it give no idea of Wolfe's lucid style. But here are a few which tell the gist of the story :

I found myself so ill, and am still so weak, that I begged the generals to consult together. They are all of opinion, that, as more ships and provisions are now got above the town, they should try, by conveying up five thousand men, to draw the enemy from his present position and bring him to an action. I have acquiesced in their proposal, and we are preparing to put

it into execution. The admiral will readily
join in any measure for the public service.
There is such a choice of difficulties that
I own myself at a loss how to determine.
The affairs of Great Britain I know require
the most vigorous measures. You may be
sure that the small part of the campaign
which remains shall be employed, as far as
I am able, for the honour of His Majesty
and the interest of the nation. I am sure
of being well seconded by the admirals and
generals; happy if our efforts here can
contribute to the success of His Majesty's
arms in any other part of America.

On the 31st, the day he wrote to his mother
and had his long talk with Saunders, Wolfe
began to send his guns and stores away from
the Montmorency camp. Carleton managed
the removal very cleverly; and on September 3
only the five thousand infantry who were to
go up the St Lawrence were left there. Wolfe
tried to tempt Montcalm to attack him. But
Montcalm knew better; and half suspected
that Wolfe himself might make another attack
on the Beauport lines. When everything was
ready, all the men at the Point of Levy who
could be spared put off in boats and rowed

over towards Beauport, just as Monckton's men had done on the disastrous last day of July. At the same time the main division of the fleet, under Saunders, made as if to support these boats, while the Levis batteries thundered against Quebec. Carleton gave the signal from the beach at Montmorency when the tide was high ; and the whole five thousand infantry marched down the hill, got into their boats, and rowed over to where the other boats were waiting. The French now prepared to defend themselves at once. But as the two divisions of boats came together, they both rowed off through the gaps between the men-of-war. Wolfe's army had broken camp and got safely away, right under the noses of the French, without the loss of a single man.

A whole week, from September 3 to 10, was then taken up with trying to see how the brigadiers' plan could be carried out.

This plan was good, as far as it went. An army is even harder to supply than a town would be if the town was taken up bodily and moved about the country. An army makes no supplies itself, but uses up a great deal. It must have food, clothing, arms, ammunition, stores of all kinds, and everything else it needs to keep it fit for action. So it must always keep what are called ' communications' with the places from which it gets these supplies. Now, Wolfe's and Montcalm's armies were both supplied along the St Lawrence, Wolfe's from below Quebec and Montcalm's from above. But Wolfe had no trouble about the safety of his own ' communications,' since they were managed and protected by the fleet. Even before he first saw Quebec, a convoy of supply ships had sailed from the Maritime Provinces for his army under the charge of a man-of-war. And so it went on all through the siege. Including forty-nine men-of-war, no less than 277 British vessels sailed up to Quebec during this campaign; and not one of them was lost on the way, though the St Lawrence had then no lighthouses, buoys, or other aids to navigation, as it has now, and though the British officers them-selves were compelled to take the ships through the worst places in these foreign and little-known waters. The result was that there were abundant supplies for the British army the whole time, thanks to the fleet.

But Montcalm was in a very different plight. Since the previous autumn, when Wolfe and Hardy had laid waste the coast of Gaspé, the supply of sea-fish had almost failed. Now the whole country below Quebec had been cut off by the fleet, while most of the country round Quebec was being laid waste by the army. Wolfe's orders were that no man, woman, or child was to be touched, nor any house or other buildings burnt, if his own men were not attacked. But if the men of the country fired at his soldiers they were to be shot down, and everything they had was to be destroyed. Of course, women and children were strictly protected, under all circumstances, and no just complaint was ever made against the British for hurting a single one. But as the men persisted in firing, the British fired back and destroyed the farms where the firing took place, on the fair-play principle that it is right to destroy whatever is used to destroy you.

It thus happened that, except at a few little villages where the men had not fired on the soldiers, the country all round Quebec was like a desert, as far as supplies for the French were concerned. The only way to obtain anything for their camp was by bringing it down the St Lawrence from Montreal, Sorel, and Three Rivers. French vessels would come down as far as they dared and then send the supplies on in barges, which kept close in under the north

shore above Quebec, where the French out-
posts and batteries protected them from the
British men-of-war that were pushing higher
and higher up the river. Some supplies were
brought in by land after they were put ashore
above the highest British vessels. But as a
hundred tons came far more easily by water than
one ton by land, it is not hard to see that Montcalm's men could not hold out long if the St
Lawrence near Quebec was closed to supplies.

Wolfe, Montcalm, the brigadiers, and every
one else on both sides knew this perfectly
well. But, as it was now September, the fleet
could not go far up the much more difficult
channel towards Montreal. If it did, and took
Wolfe's army with it, the few French men-of-
war might dispute the passage, and some
sunken ships might block the way, at all
events for a time. Besides, the French were
preparing to repulse any landing up the river,
between Cap Rouge, nine miles above Quebec,
and Deschambault, forty miles above ; and
with good prospect of success, because the
country favoured their irregulars. Moreover,
if Wolfe should land many miles up, Montcalm
might still hold out far down in Quebec for the
few days remaining till October. If, on the
other hand, the fleet went up and left Wolfe's

men behind, Montcalm would be safer than ever at Beauport and Quebec ; because, how could Wolfe reach him without a fleet when he had failed to reach him with one ?

The life-and-death question for Wolfe was how to land close enough above Quebec and soon enough in September to make Montcalm fight it out on even terms and in the open field.

The brigadiers' plan of landing high up seemed all right till they tried to work it out. Then they found troubles in plenty. There were several places for them to land between Cap Rouge, nine miles above Quebec, and Pointe-aux-Trembles, thirteen miles higher still. Ever since July 18 British vessels had been passing to and fro above Quebec ; and in August, Murray, under the guard of Holmes's squadron, had tried his brigade against Pointe-aux-Trembles, where he was beaten back, and at Deschambault, twenty miles farther up, where he took some prisoners and burnt some supplies. To ward off further and perhaps more serious attacks from this quarter, Montcalm had been keeping Bougainville on the lookout, especially round Pointe-aux-Trembles, for several weeks before the brigadiers arranged their plan. Bougainville now had 2000 in-

fantry, all the mounted men—nearly 300—
and all the best Indian and Canadian scouts,
along the thirteen miles of shore between Cap
Rouge and Pointe-aux-Trembles. His land and
water batteries had also been made much
stronger. He and Montcalm were in close
touch and could send messages to each
other and get an answer back within four
hours.

On the 7th Wolfe and the brigadiers had
a good look at every spot round Pointe-aux-
Trembles. On the 8th and 9th the brigadiers
were still there ; while five transports sailed
past Quebec on the 8th to join Holmes, who
commanded the up-river squadron. Two of
Wolfe's brigades were now on board the
transports with Holmes. But the whole three
were needed ; and this need at once entailed
another difficulty. A successful landing on
the north shore above Quebec could only be
made under cover of the dark ; and Wolfe
could not bring the third brigade, under cover
of night, from the island of Orleans and the
Point of Levy, and land it with the other two
twenty miles up the river before daylight.
The tidal stream runs up barely five hours,
while it runs down more than seven ; and
winds are mostly down. Next, if, instead

of sailing, the third brigade marched twenty miles at night across very rough country on the south shore, it would arrive later than ever. Then, only one brigade could be put ashore in boats at one time in one place, and Bougainville could collect enough men to hold it in check while he called in reinforcements at least as fast on the French side as the British could on theirs. Another thing was that the wooded country favoured the French defence and hindered the British attack. Lastly, if Wolfe and Saunders collected the whole five thousand soldiers and a still larger squadron and convoy up the river, Montcalm would see the men and ships being moved from their positions in front of his Beauport entrenchments, and would hurry to the threatened shore between Cap Rouge and Pointe-aux-Trembles almost as soon as the British, and certainly in time to reinforce Bougainville and repulse Wolfe.

The 9th was Wolfe's last Sunday. It was a cheerless, rainy day ; and he almost confessed himself beaten for good, as he sat writing his last official letter to one of Pitt's friends, the Earl of Holderness. He dated it, ' On board the *Sutherland* at anchor off Cap Rouge, September 9, 1759.' He ended it with gloomy news : ' I am so far recovered as to be able to do business, but my constitution is entirely ruined, without the consolation of having done any considerable service to the state, or without any prospect of it.'

The very next day, however, he saw his chance.   He stood at Etchemin, on the south shore, two miles above Quebec, and looked long and earnestly through his telescope at the Foulon road, a mile and a half away, running up to the Plains of Abraham from the Anse au Foulon, which has ever since been called Wolfe's Cove.   Then he looked at the Plains themselves, especially at a spot only one mile from Quebec, where the flat and open ground formed a perfect field of battle for his well-drilled regulars.   He knew the Foulon road must be fairly good, because it was the French line of communication between the Anse au Foulon and the Beauport camp. The Cove and the nearest point of the camp were only two miles and a quarter apart, as the crow flies.   But between them rose the tableland of the Plains, 300 feet above the river.   Thus they were screened from each other, and a surprise at the Cove might not be found out too soon at the camp.

Now, Wolfe knew that the French expected

to be attacked either above Cap Rouge (up towards Pointe-aux-Trembles) or below Quebec (down in their Beauport entrenchments). He also knew that his own army thought the attack would be made above Cap Rouge. Thus the French were still very anxious about the six miles at Beauport, while both sides were keenly watching each other all over the thirteen miles above Cap Rouge. Nobody seemed to be thinking about the nine miles between Cap Rouge and Quebec, and least of all about the part nearest Quebec.

Yes, one man was thinking about it, and he never stopped thinking about it till he died. That man was Montcalm. On the 5th, when Wolfe began moving up-stream, Montcalm had sent a whole battalion to the Plains. But on the 7th, when the British generals were all at Pointe-aux-Trembles, Vaudreuil, always ready to spite Montcalm, ordered this battalion back to camp, saying, ' The British haven't got wings ; they can't fly up to the Plains ! ' Wolfe, of course, saw that the battalion had been taken away ; and he soon found out why. Vaudreuil was a great talker and could never keep a secret. Wolfe knew perfectly well that Vaudreuil and Bigot were constantly spoiling whatever Montcalm was doing, so he counted on this trouble in the French camp as he did on other facts and chances.

He now gave up all idea of his old plans against Beauport, as well as the new plan of the brigadiers, and decided on another plan of his own. It was new in one way, because he had never seen a chance of carrying it out before. But it was old in another way, because he had written to his uncle from Louisbourg on May 19, and spoken of getting up the heights four or five miles above Quebec if he could do so by surprise. Again, even so early in the siege as July 18 he had been chafing at what he called the ' coldness ' of the fleet about pushing up beyond Quebec. The entry in his private diary for that day is : ' The *Sutherland* and *Squirrell*, two transports, and two armed sloops passed the narrow passage between Quebec and Levy *without losing a man.*' Next day, his entry is more scathing still : ' Reconnoitred the country immediately above Quebec and found that *if we had ventured the stroke that was first intended we should infallibly have succeeded.*' This shows how long he had kept the plan waiting for the chance. But it does not prove that he had missed any earlier chances through the ' coldness ' of the fleet. For it is significant that he afterwards struck

out '*infallibly*' and substituted '*probably*';
while it must be remembered that the *Sutherland* and her consorts formed only a very small
flotilla, that they passed Quebec in the middle
of a very dark night, that the St Lawrence
above the town was intricate and little known,
that the loss of several men-of-war might
have been fatal, that the enemy's attention
had not become distracted in July to anything
like the same bewildering extent as it had in
September, and that the intervening course
of events—however disappointing in itself—
certainly helped to make his plan suit the
occasion far better late than soon. Moreover, in a note to Saunders in August, he had
spoken about a ' desperate ' plan which he
could not trust his brigadiers to carry out, and
which he was then too sick to carry out himself.

Now that he was ' patched up ' enough for
a few days, and that the chance seemed to
be within his grasp, he made up his mind
to strike at once. He knew that the little
French post above the Anse au Foulon was
commanded by one of Bigot's blackguards,
Vergor, whose Canadian militiamen were as
slack as their commander. He knew that
the Samos battery, a little farther from Quebec,

had too small a garrison, with only five guns
and no means of firing them on the landward
side; so that any of his men, once up the
heights, could rush it from the rear. He
knew the French had only a few weak posts
the whole way down from Cap Rouge, and
that these posts often let convoys of provision
boats pass quietly at night into the Anse au
Foulon. He knew that some of Montcalm's
best regulars had gone to Montreal with
Lévis, the excellent French second-in-command, to strengthen the defence against
Amherst's slow advance from Lake Champlain.
He knew that Montcalm still had a total of
10,000 men between Montmorency and Quebec,
as against his own attacking force of 5000;
yet he also knew that the odds of two to one
were reversed in his favour so far as European
regulars were concerned; for Montcalm could
not now bring 3000 French regulars into
immediate action at any one spot. Finally,
he knew that all the French were only half-fed,
and that those with Bougainville were getting
worn out by having to march across country,
in a fruitless effort to keep pace with the ships
of Holmes's squadron and convoy, which
floated up and down with the tide.

Wolfe's plan was to keep the French alarmed

more than ever at the two extreme ends of
their line—Beauport below Quebec and Pointe-
aux-Trembles above—and then to strike home
at their undefended centre, by a surprise landing at the Anse au Foulon. Once landed,
well before daylight, he could rush Vergor's
post and the Samos battery, march across the
Plains, and form his line of battle a mile
from Quebec before Montcalm could come up
in force from Beauport. Probably he could also
defeat him before Bougainville could march
down from some point well above Cap Rouge.

There were chances to reckon with in this
plan. But so there are in all plans; and
to say Wolfe took Quebec by mere luck is
utter nonsense. He was one of the deepest
thinkers on war who ever lived, especially on
the British kind of war, by land and sea together ; and he had had the preparation of a
lifetime to help him in using a fleet and army
that worked together like the two arms of one
body. He simply made a plan which took
proper account of all the facts and all the
chances. Fools make lucky hits, now and
then, by the merest chance. But no one except
a genius can make and carry out a plan like
Wolfe's, which meant at least a hundred hits
running, all in the selfsame spot.

No sooner had Wolfe made his admirable plan that Monday morning, September 10, than he set all the principal officers to work out the different parts of it. But he kept the whole a secret. Nobody except himself knew more than one part, and how that one part was to be worked in at the proper time and place. Even the fact that the Anse au Foulon was to be the landing-place was kept secret till the last moment from everybody except Admiral Holmes, who made all the arrangements, and Captain Chads, the naval officer who was to lead the first boats down. The great plot thickened fast. The siege that had been an affair of weeks, and the brigadiers' plan that had been an affair of days, both gave way to a plan in which every hour was made to tell. Wolfe's seventy hours of consummate manœuvres, by land and water, over a front of thirty miles, were followed by a battle in which the fighting of only a few minutes settled the fate of Canada for centuries.

During the whole of those momentous three days—Monday, Tuesday, and Wednesday, September 10, 11, and 12, 1759—Wolfe, Saunders, and Holmes kept the French in constant alarm about the thirteen miles *above* Cap Rouge and the six miles *below* Quebec; but gave no sign by which any immediate danger could be suspected along the nine miles *between* Cap Rouge and Quebec.

Saunders stayed below Quebec. On the 12th he never gave the French a minute's rest all day and night. He sent Cook and others close in towards Beauport to lay buoys, as if to mark out a landing-place for another attack like the one on July 31. It is a singular co-incidence that while Cook, the great British circumnavigator of the globe, was trying to get Wolfe into Quebec, Bougainville, the great French circumnavigator, was trying to keep him out. Towards evening Saunders formed up his boats and filled them with marines, whose own red coats, seen at a distance, made them look like soldiers. He moved his fleet in at high tide and fired furiously at the entrench-ments. All night long his boatloads of men rowed up and down and kept the French on the alert. This feint against Beauport was much helped by the men of Wolfe's third brigade, who remained at the island of Orleans and the Point of Levy till after dark, by a whole battalion of marines guarding the Levis batteries, and by these batteries themselves, which, meanwhile, were bombarding Quebec—again like the 31st of July. The bombardment was kept up all night and became most intense just before dawn, when Wolfe was landing two miles above.

At the other end of the French line, above Cap Rouge, Holmes had kept threatening Bougainville more and more towards Pointe-aux-Trembles, twenty miles above the Foulon. Wolfe's soldiers had kept landing on the south shore day after day; then drifting up with the tide on board the transports past Pointe-aux-Trembles; then drifting down towards Cap Rouge; and then coming back the next day to do the same thing over again. This had been going on, more or less, even before Wolfe had made his plan, and it proved very useful to him. He knew that Bougainville's men were getting quite worn out by scrambling across country, day after day, to keep up with Holmes's restless squadron and transports. He also knew that men who threw themselves down, tired out, late at night could not be collected from different places, all over their thirteen-mile beat, and brought down in the morning, fit to fight on a battlefield eight miles from the nearest of them and twenty-one from the farthest.

Montcalm was greatly troubled. He saw redcoats with Saunders opposite Beauport,

redcoats at the island, redcoats at the Point of
Levy, and redcoats guarding the Levis batteries.
He had no means of finding out at once that
the redcoats with Saunders and at the batteries
were marines, and that the redcoats who really
did belong to Wolfe were under orders to
march off after dark that very night and join
the other two brigades which were coming
down the river from the squadron above Cap
Rouge. He had no boats that could get
through the perfect screen of the British fleet.
But all that the skill of mortal man could do
against these odds he did on that fatal eve of
battle, as he had done for three years past, with
foes in front and false friends behind. He
ordered the battalion which he had sent to the
Plains on the 5th, and which Vaudreuil had
brought back on the 7th, 'now to go and camp
at the Foulon'; that is, at the top of the road
coming up from Wolfe's landing-place at the
Anse au Foulon. But Vaudreuil immediately
gave a counter-order and said: 'We'll see
about that to-morrow.' Vaudreuil's 'to-
morrow' never came.

That afternoon of the 12th, while Montcalm and Vaudreuil were at cross-purposes
near the mouth of the St Charles, Wolfe was
only four miles away, on the other side of the

Plains, in a boat on the St Lawrence, where he was taking his last look at what he then called the Foulon and what the world now calls Wolfe's Cove. His boat was just turning to drift up in midstream, off Sillery Point, which is only half a mile above the Foulon. He wanted to examine the Cove well through his telescope at dead low tide, as he intended to land his army there at the next low tide. Close beside him sat young Robison, who was not an officer in either the Army or Navy, but who had come out to Canada as tutor to an admiral's son, and who had been found so good at maps that he was employed with Wolfe's engineers in making surveys and sketches of the ground about Quebec. Shutting up his telescope, Wolfe sat silent a while. Then, as afterwards recorded by Robison, he turned towards his officers and repeated several stanzas of Gray's *Elegy*. 'Gentlemen,' he said as he ended, 'I would sooner have written that poem than beat the French to-morrow.' He did not know then that his own fame would far surpass the poet's, and that he should win it in the very way described in one of the lines he had just been quoting—

The paths of glory lead but to the grave.

At half-past eight in the evening he was sitting in his cabin on board Holmes's flag-ship, the *Sutherland*, above Cap Rouge, with ' Jacky Jervis '—the future Earl St Vincent, but now the youngest captain in the fleet, only twenty-four.   Wolfe and Jervis had both been at the same school at Greenwich, Swinden's, though at different times, and they were great friends.   Wolfe had made up a sealed parcel of his notebook, his will, and the portrait of Katherine Lowther, and he now handed it over to Jervis for safe keeping.

But he had no chance of talking about old times at home, for just then a letter from the three brigadiers was handed in.   It asked him if he would not give them ' distinct orders ' about ' the place or places we are to attack.' He wrote back to the senior, Monckton, telling him what he had arranged for the first and second brigades, and then, separately, to Townshend about the third, which was not with Holmes but on the south shore.   After dark the men from the island and the Point of Levy had marched up to join this brigade at Etchemin, the very place where Wolfe had made his plan on the 10th, as he stood and looked at the Foulon opposite.

His last general orders to his army had been

read out some hours before; but, of course, the Foulon was not mentioned. These orders show that he well understood the great issues he was fighting for, and what men he had to count upon. Here are only three sentences; but how much they mean! 'The enemy's force is now divided. A vigorous blow struck by the army at this juncture may determine the fate of Canada. The officers and men will remember what their country expects of them.' The watchword was 'Coventry,' which, being probably suggested by the saying, 'Sent to Coventry,' that is, condemned to silence, was as apt a word for this expectant night as 'Gibraltar,' the symbol of strength, was for the one on which Quebec surrendered.

Just before dark Holmes sent every vessel he could spare to make a show of force opposite Pointe-aux-Trembles, in order to hold Bougainville there overnight. But after dark the main body of Holmes's squadron and all the boats and small transports came together opposite Cap Rouge. Just before ten a single lantern appeared in the *Sutherland's* main topmast shrouds. On seeing this, Chads formed up the boats between the ships and the south shore, the side away from the French. In three hours every man was in his place. Not a sound was to be heard except the murmur of the strong ebb-tide setting down towards Quebec and a gentle south-west breeze blowing in the same direction. ' All ready, sir ! ' and Wolfe took his own place in the first boat with his friend Captain Delaune, the leader of the twenty-four men of the 'Forlorn Hope,' who were to be the first to scale the cliff. Then a second lantern appeared above the first ; and the whole brigade of boats began to move off in succession. They had about eight miles to go. But the current ran the distance in two hours. As they advanced they could see the flashes from the Levis batteries growing brighter and more frequent ; for both the land gunners there and the seamen gunners with Saunders farther down were increasing their fire as the hour for Wolfe's landing drew near.

A couple of miles above the Foulon the *Hunter* was anchored in midstream. As arranged, Chads left the south shore and steered straight for her. To his surprise he saw her crew training their guns on him. But they held their fire. Then Wolfe came alongside and found that she had two French deserters on board who had mistaken his boats for the French provision convoy that was expected to creep down the north shore

that very night and land at the Foulon.
He had already planned to pass his boats off
as this convoy; for he knew that the farthest
up of Holmes's men-of-war had stopped it
above Pointe-aux-Trembles. But he was glad
to know that the French posts below Cap
Rouge had not yet heard of the stoppage.

From the *Hunter* his boat led the way to
Sillery Point, half a mile above the Foulon.
'Halt!   Who comes there!'—a French
sentry's voice rang out in the silence of the
night. 'France!' answered young Fraser,
who had been taken into Wolfe's boat because
he spoke French like a native. 'What's your
regiment?' asked the sentry. 'The Queen's,'
answered Fraser, who knew that this was the
one supplying the escort for the provision boats
the British had held up. 'But why don't you
speak out?' asked the sentry again. 'Hush!'
said Fraser, 'the British will hear us if you
make a noise.' And there, sure enough,
was the *Hunter*, drifting down, as arranged, not
far outside the column of boats. Then the
sentry let them all pass; and, in ten minutes
more, exactly at four o'clock, the leading boat
grounded in the Anse au Foulon and Wolfe
jumped ashore.

He at once took the 'Forlorn Hope' and 200

light infantry to the side of the Cove towards
Quebec, saying as he went, 'I don't know if we
shall all get up, but we must make the attempt.'
Then, while these men were scrambling up,
he went back to the middle of the Cove, where
Howe had already formed the remaining 500
light infantry. Captain Macdonald, a very
active climber, passed the 'Forlorn Hope' and
was the first man to reach the top and feel
his way through the trees to the left, towards
Vergor's tents. Presently he almost ran into
the sleepy French-Canadian sentry, who heard
only a voice speaking perfect French and telling
him it was all right—nothing but the reinforcements from the Beauport camp; for
Wolfe knew that Montcalm had been trying to
get a French regular officer to replace Vergor,
who was as good a thief as Bigot and as bad a
soldier as Vaudreuil. While this little parley
was going on the 'Forlorn Hope' came up;
when Macdonald promptly hit the sentry between the eyes with the hilt of his claymore
and knocked him flat. The light infantry
pressed on close behind. The dumbfounded
French colonial troops coming out of their
tents found themselves face to face with a
whole woodful of fixed bayonets. They fired
a few shots. The British charged with a loud

cheer. The Canadians scurried away through the trees. And Vergor ran for dear life in his nightshirt.

The ringing cheer with which Delaune charged home told Wolfe at the foot of the road that the actual top was clear. Then Howe went up; and in fifteen minutes all the light infantry had joined their comrades above. Another battalion followed quickly, and Wolfe himself followed them. By this time it was five o'clock and quite light. The boats that had landed the first brigade had already rowed through the gaps between the small transports which were landing the second brigade, and had reached the south shore, a mile and a half away, where the third brigade was waiting for them.

Meanwhile the suddenly roused gunners of the Samos battery were firing wildly at the British vessels. But the men-of-war fired back with better aim, and Howe's light infantry, coming up at a run from behind, dashed in among the astonished gunners with the bayonet, cleared them all out, and spiked every gun. Howe left three companies there to hold the battery against Bougainville later in the day, and returned with the other seven to Wolfe. It was now six o'clock. The third brigade had landed, the whole of the ground at the top was clear; and Wolfe set off with 1000 men to see what Montcalm was doing.

Quebec stands on the eastern end of a sort of promontory, or narrow tableland, between the St Lawrence and the valley of the St Charles. This tableland is less than a mile wide and narrows still more as it approaches Quebec. Its top is tilted over towards the St Charles and Beauport, the cliffs being only 100 feet high there, instead of 300, as they are beside the St Lawrence; so Wolfe, as he turned in towards Quebec, after marching straight across the tableland, could look out over the French camp. Everything seemed quiet; so he made his left secure and sent for his main body to follow him at once. It was now seven. In another hour his line of battle was formed, his reserves had taken post in his rear, and a brigade of seamen from Saunders's fleet were landing guns, stores, blankets, tents, entrenching tools, and whatever else he would need for besieging the city after defeating Montcalm. The 3000 sailors on the beach were anything but pleased with the tame work of waiting there while the soldiers were fighting up above. One of their officers, in a letter home, said they could hardly stand still, and were perpetually swearing because they were not allowed to get into the heat of action.

The whole of the complicated manœuvres, in face of an active enemy, for three days and three nights, by land and water, over a front of thirty miles, had now been crowned by complete success. The army of 5000 men had been put ashore at the right time and in the right way; and it was now ready to fight one of the great immortal battles of the world.

'The thin red line.' The phrase was invented long after Wolfe's day. But Wolfe invented the fact. The six battalions which formed his front, that thirteenth morning of September 1759, were drawn up in the first two-deep line that ever stood on any field of battle in the world since war began. And it was Wolfe alone who made this 'thin red line,' as surely as it was Wolfe alone who made the plan that conquered Canada.

Meanwhile Montcalm had not been idle; though he was perplexed to the last, because one of the stupid rules in the French camp was that all news was to be told first to Vaudreuil, who, as governor-general, could pass it on or not, and interfere with the army as much as he liked. When it was light enough to see

Saunders's fleet, the island of Orleans, and the Point of Levy, Montcalm at once noticed that Wolfe's men had gone. He galloped down to the bridge of boats, where he found that Vaudreuil had already heard of Wolfe's landing. At first the French thought the firing round the Foulon was caused by an exchange of shots between the Samos battery and some British men-of-war that were trying to stop the French provision boats from getting in there. But Vergor's fugitives and the French patrols near Quebec soon told the real story. And then, just before seven, Montcalm himself caught sight of Wolfe's first redcoats marching in along the Ste Foy road. Well might he exclaim, after all he had done and Vaudreuil had undone : ' There they are, where they have no right to be ! '

He at once sent orders, all along his six miles of entrenchments, to bring up every French regular and all the rest except 2000 militia. But Vaudreuil again interfered ; and Montcalm got only the French and Canadian regulars, 2500, and the same number of Canadian militia with a few Indians. The French and British totals, actually present on the field of battle, were, therefore, almost exactly equal, 5000 each. Vaudreuil also forgot to order out the field guns, the horses for which the vile and corrupt Bigot had been using for himself. At nine Montcalm had formed up his French and colonial regulars between Quebec and the crest of rising ground across the Plains beyond which lay Wolfe. Riding forward till he could see the redcoats, he noticed how thin their line was on its left and in its centre, and that its right, near the St Lawrence, had apparently not formed at all. But his eye deceived him about the British right, as the men were lying down there, out of sight, behind a swell of ground. He galloped back and asked if any one had further news. Several officers declared they had heard that Wolfe was entrenching, but that his right brigade had not yet had time to march on to the field. There was no possible way of finding out anything else at once. The chance seemed favourable. Montcalm knew he had to fight or starve, as he was completely cut off by land and water, except for one bad, swampy road in the valley of the St Charles ; and he ordered his line to advance.

At half-past nine the French reached the crest and halted. The two armies were now in full view of each other on the Plains and only a quarter of a mile apart. The French

line of battle had eight small battalions, about
2500 men, formed six deep. The colonial
regulars, in three battalions, were on the
flanks. The five battalions of French regulars
were in the centre. Montcalm, wearing a
green and gold uniform, with the brilliant
cross of St Louis over his cuirass, and mounted
on a splendid black charger, rode the whole
length of his line, to see if all were ready to
attack. The French regulars—half-fed, sorely
harassed, interfered with by Vaudreuil—were
still the victors of Ticonderoga, against the
British odds of four to one. Perhaps they
might snatch one last desperate victory from
the fortunes of war ? Certainly all would
follow wherever they were led by their beloved
Montcalm, the greatest Frenchman of the
whole New World. He said a few stirring
words to each of his well-known regiments as
he rode by ; and when he laughingly asked the
best of all, the Royal Roussillon, if they were
not tired enough to take a little rest before the
battle, they shouted back that they were never
too tired to fight—' Forward, forward ! ' And
their steady blue ranks, and those of the four
white regiments beside them, with bayonets
fixed and colours flying, did indeed look fit
and ready for the fray.

Wolfe also had gone along his line of battle, the first of all two-deep thin red lines, to make sure that every officer understood the order that there was to be no firing until the French came close up, to within only forty paces. As soon as he saw Montcalm's line on the crest he had moved his own a hundred paces forward, according to previous arrangement; so that the two enemies were now only a long musket - shot apart. The Canadians and Indians were pressing round the British flanks, under cover of the bushes, and firing hard. But they were easily held in check by the light infantry on the left rear of the line and by the 35th on the right rear. The few French and British skirmishers in the centre now ran back to their own lines; and before ten the field was quite clear between the two opposing fronts.

Wolfe had been wounded twice when going along his line; first in the wrist and then in the groin. Yet he stood up so straight and looked so cool that when he came back to take post on the right the men there did not know he had been hit at all. His spirit already soared in triumph over the weakness of the flesh. Here he was, a sick and doubly wounded man; but a soldier, a hero, and a conqueror,

with the key to half a continent almost within
his eager grasp.

At a signal from Montcalm in the centre
the French line advanced about a hundred
yards in perfect formation. Then the Canadian regulars suddenly began firing without
orders, and threw themselves flat on the
ground to reload. By the time they had got
up the French regulars had halted some distance in front of them, fired a volley, and
begun advancing again. This was too much
for the Canadians. Though they were regulars
they were not used to fighting in the open,
not trained for it, and not armed for it with
bayonets. In a couple of minutes they had all
slunk off to the flanks and joined the Indians
and militia, who were attacking the British
from under cover.

This left the French regulars face to face
with Wolfe's front : five French battalions
against the British six. These two fronts were
now to decide the fate of Canada between
them. The French still came bravely on ;
but their six-deep line was much shorter than
the British two-deep line, and they saw that
both their flanks were about to be over-lapped
by fire and steel. They inclined outwards to
save themselves from this fatal overlap on

both right and left. But that made just as
fatal a gap in their centre. Their whole line
wavered, halted oftener to fire, and fired more
wildly at each halt.

In the meantime Wolfe's front stood firm
as a rock and silent as the grave, one long,
straight, living wall of red, with the double
line of deadly keen bayonets glittering above
it. Nothing stirred along its whole length,
except the Union Jacks, waving defiance at
the fleurs-de-lis, and those patient men who
fell before a fire to which they could not
yet reply. Bayonet after bayonet would
suddenly flash out of line and fall forward,
as the stricken redcoat, standing there with
shouldered arms, quivered and sank to the
ground.

Captain York had brought up a single gun
in time for the battle, the sailors having
dragged it up the cliff and run it the whole
way across the Plains. He had been handling
it most gallantly during the French advance,
firing showers of grape-shot into their ranks
from a position right out in the open in front
of Wolfe's line. But now that the French were
closing he had to retire. The sailors then
picked up the drag-ropes and romped in with
this most effective six-pounder at full speed, as

if they were having the greatest fun of their lives.

Wolfe was standing next to the Louis-bourg Grenadiers, who, this time, were determined not to begin before they were told. He was to give their colonel the signal to fire the first volley; which then was itself to be the signal for a volley from each of the other five battalions, one after another, all down the line. Every musket was loaded with two bullets, and the moment a battalion had fired it was to advance twenty paces, loading as it went, and then fire a ' general,' that is, each man for himself, as hard as he could, till the bugles sounded the charge.

Wolfe now watched every step the French line made. Nearer and nearer it came. A hundred paces ! — seventy - five ! — fifty !— forty ! !—*Fire ! ! !* Crash ! came the volley from the grenadiers. Five volleys more rang out in quick succession, all so perfectly delivered that they sounded more like six great guns than six battalions with hundreds of muskets in each. Under cover of the smoke Wolfe's men advanced their twenty paces and halted to fire the ' general.' The dense, six-deep lines of Frenchmen reeled, staggered, and seemed to melt away under this awful

deluge of lead. In five minutes their right
was shaken out of all formation. All that
remained of it turned and fled, a wild, mad
mob of panic-stricken fugitives. The centre
followed at once. But the Royal Roussillon
stood fast a little longer ; and when it also
turned it had only three unwounded officers
left, and they were trying to rally it.

Montcalm, who had led the centre and had
been wounded in the advance, galloped over to
the Royal Roussillon as it was making this last
stand. But even he could not stem the rush
that followed and that carried him along with
it. Over the crest and down to the valley of
the St Charles his army fled, the Canadians
and Indians scurrying away through the bushes
as hard as they could run. While making
one more effort to rally enough men to cover
the retreat he was struck again, this time by
a dozen grape-shot from York's gun. He
reeled in the saddle. But two of his grenadiers caught him and held him up while he
rode into Quebec. As he passed through St
Louis Gate a terrified woman called out, ' Oh !
look at the marquis, he 's killed, he 's killed ! '
But Montcalm, by a supreme effort, sat up
straight for a moment and said : ' It is nothing
at all, my kind friend ; you must not be so

much alarmed!' and, saying this, passed on
to die, a hero to the very last.

In the thick of the short, fierce fire-fight
the bagpipes began to skirl, the Highlanders
dashed down their muskets, drew their claymores, and gave a yell that might have been
heard across the river. In a moment every
British bugle was sounding the 'Charge' and
the whole red, living wall was rushing forward
with a roaring cheer.

But it charged without Wolfe. He had
been mortally wounded just after giving the
signal for those famous volleys. Two officers
sprang to his side. 'Hold me up!' he im-
plored them, 'don't let my gallant fellows see
me fall!' With the help of a couple of men
he was carried back to the far side of a little
knoll and seated on a grenadier's folded coat,
while the grenadier who had taken it off ran
over to a spring to get some water. Wolfe
knew at once that he was dying. But he did
not yet know how the battle had gone. His
head had sunk on his breast, and his eyes were
already glazing, when an officer on the knoll
called out, 'They run! They run! 'Egad,
they give way everywhere!' Rousing himself, as if from sleep, Wolfe asked, 'Who
run?'—'The French, sir!'—'Then I die

content ! '—and, almost as he said it, he breathed his last.

He was not buried on the field he won, nor even in the country that he conquered. All that was mortal of him—his poor, sick, wounded body—was borne back across the sea, and carried in mourning triumph through his native land. And there, in the family vault at Greenwich, near the school he had left for his first war, half his short life ago, he was laid to rest on November 20—at the very time when his own great victory before Quebec was being confirmed by Hawke's magnificently daring attack on the French fleet amid all the dangers of that wild night in Quiberon Bay.

Canada has none of his mortality. But could she have anything more sacred than the spot from which his soaring spirit took its flight into immortal fame ? And could this sacred spot be marked by any words more winged than these :

HERE DIED
WOLFE
VICTORIOUS

CHAPTER VIII

EPILOGUE—THE LAST STAND

WOLFE'S victory on the Plains of Abraham proved decisive in the end; but it was not the last of the great struggle for the Key of Canada.

After Wolfe had died on the field of battle, and Monckton had been disabled by his wounds, Townshend took command, received the surrender of Quebec on the 18th, and waited till the French field army had retired towards Montreal. Then he sailed home with Saunders, leaving Murray to hold what Wolfe had won. Saunders left Lord Colville in charge of a strong squadron, with orders to wait at Halifax till the spring.

Both French and British spent a terrible winter. The French had better shelter in Montreal than the British had among the ruins of Quebec; and, being more accustomed to the rigours of the climate, they would have suffered less from cold in any case. But their lot was, on the whole, the harder of the two;

THE DEATH OF WOLFE

After the painting by Benjamin West

for food was particularly bad and scarce in
Montreal, where even horseflesh was thought a
luxury. Both armies were ravaged by disease
to a most alarming extent. Of the eight
thousand men with whom Murray began that
deadly winter not one-half were able to bear
arms in the spring ; and not one-half of those
who did bear arms then were really fit for
duty.

Montcalm's successor, Lévis, now made a
skilful, bold, and gallant attempt to retake
Quebec before navigation opened. Calling the
whole remaining strength of New France to
his aid, he took his army down in April, mostly
by way of the St Lawrence. The weather was
stormy. The banks of the river were lined
with rotting ice. The roads were almost im-
passable. Yet, after a journey of less than
ten days, the whole French army appeared
before Quebec. Murray was at once con-
fronted by a dire dilemma. The landward
defences had never been strong ; and he had
not been able to do more than patch them up.
If he remained behind them Lévis would close
in, batter them down, and probably carry them
by assault against a sickly garrison depressed
by being kept within the walls. If, on the
other hand, he marched out, he would have

to meet more than double numbers at the
least; for some men would have to be left
to cover a retreat; and he knew the French
grand total was nearly thrice his own. But
he chose this bolder course; and at the chill
dawn of April 28, he paraded his little
attacking force of a bare three thousand
men on the freezing snow and mud of the
Esplanade and then marched out.

The two armies met at Ste Foy, a mile and
a half beyond the walls; and a desperate
battle ensued. The French had twice as
many men in action, but only half of these were
regulars; the others had no bayonets; and
there was no effective artillery to keep down
the fire of Murray's commanding guns. The
terrific fight went on for hours, while victory
inclined neither to one side nor the other. It
was a far more stubborn and much bloodier
contest than Wolfe's of the year before. At
last a British battalion was fairly caught in
flank by overwhelming numbers and driven
across the front of Murray's guns, whose pro-
tecting fire it thus completely masked at a
most critical time. Murray thereupon ordered
up his last reserve. But even so he could no
longer stand his ground. Slowly and sullenly
his exhausted men fell back before the French,

who put the very last ounce of their own failing
strength into a charge that took the guns.
Then the beaten British staggered in behind
their walls, while the victorious French stood
fast, worn out by the hardships of their march
and fought to a standstill in the battle.

Lévis rallied his army for one more effort
and pressed the siege to the uttermost of his
power. Murray had lost a thousand men and
could now muster less than three thousand.
Each side prepared to fight the other to the
death. But both knew that the result would
depend on the fleets. There had been no news
from Europe since navigation closed; and
hopes ran high among the besiegers that
perhaps some friendly men-of-war might still
be first; when of course Quebec would have
to surrender at discretion, and Canada would
certainly be saved for France if the half-
expected peace would only follow soon.

Day after day all eyes, both French and
British, looked seaward from the heights and
walls; though fleets had never yet been known
to come up the St Lawrence so early in the
season. At last, on May 9, the tops of a
man-of-war were sighted just beyond the
Point of Levy. Either she or Quebec, or
both, might have false colours flying. So

neither besiegers nor besieged knew to which side she belonged. Nor did she know herself whether Quebec was French or British. Slowly she rounded into the harbour, her crew at quarters, her decks all cleared for action. She saluted with twenty-one guns and swung out her captain's barge. Then, for the first time, every one watching knew what she was; for the barge was heading straight in towards the town, and redcoats and bluejackets could see each other plainly. In a moment every British soldier who could stand had climbed the nearest wall and was cheering her to the echo; while the gunners showed their delight by loading and firing as fast as possible and making all the noise they could.

But one ship was not enough to turn the scale; and Lévis redoubled his efforts. On the night of the 15th French hopes suddenly flared up all through the camp when the word flew round that three strange men-of-war just reported down off Beauport were the vanguard of a great French fleet. But daylight showed them to be British, and British bent on immediate and vigorous attack. Two of these frigates made straight for the French flotilla, which fled in wild confusion, covered by the undaunted Vauquelin in the *Atalante*, which fought a

LORD AMHERST

From the painting by Sir Joshua Reynolds

gallant rearguard action all the twenty miles to Pointe-aux-Trembles, where she was driven ashore and forced to strike her colours, after another, and still more desperate, resistance of over two hours. That night Lévis raised the siege in despair and retired on Montreal. Next morning Lord Colville arrived with the main body of the fleet, having made the earliest ascent of the St Lawrence ever known to naval history, before that time or since.

Then came the final scene of all this moving drama. Step by step overpowering British forces closed in on the doomed and dwindling army of New France. They closed in from east and west and south, each one of their converging columns more than a match for all that was left of the French. Whichever way he looked, Lévis could see no loophole of escape. There was nothing but certain defeat in front and on both flanks, and starvation in the rear. So when the advancing British met, all together, at the island of Montreal, he and his faithful regulars laid down their arms without dishonour, in the fully justifiable belief that no further use of them could possibly retrieve the great lost cause of France in Canada.

BIBLIOGRAPHICAL NOTE

WOLFE is one of the great heroes in countless books of modern British history, by far the greatest hero in the many books about the fight for Canada, and the single hero of four biographies. It was more than a century after his triumphant death before the first of these appeared: *The Life of Major-General James Wolfe* by Robert Wright. A second Life of Wolfe appeared a generation later, this time in the form of a small volume by A. G. Bradley in the 'English Men of Action' series. The third and fourth biographies were both published in 1909, the year which marked the third jubilee of the Battle of the Plains. One of them, Edward Salmon's *General Wolfe*, devotes more than the usual perfunctory attention to the important influence of sea-power; but it is a sketch rather than a complete biography, and it is by no means free from error. The other is *The Life and Letters of James Wolfe* by Beckles Willson.

The histories written with the best knowledge of Wolfe's career in Canada are: the contemporary *Journal of the Campaigns in North America* by Captain John Knox, Parkman's *Montcalm and Wolfe*, and *The Siege of Quebec and the Battle of the Plains of Abraham* by A. G. Doughty and G. W. Parmelee. Knox's two very scarce quarto volumes have been edited by A. G. Doughty for the Champlain Society for republication in 1914. Parkman's work is always excellent. But he wrote before seeing some of the evidence so admirably revealed in Dr Doughty's six volumes, and, like the rest, he failed to understand the real value of the fleet.

INDEX

Printed by T. and A. Constable, Printers to His Majesty
at the Edinburgh University Press

CHRONICLES OF CANADA

Edited by George M. Wrong and H. H. Langton
of the University of Toronto

A series of thirty-two tersely-written narratives for popular reading, designed to set forth, in historic continuity, the principal events and movements in Canada, from the Earliest Explorers to the Railway Builders.

* NOTE.—The eight volumes marked with an asterisk are still in preparation and subject to changes in authorship should unforeseen circumstances prevent any author from completing his manuscript.

Published by
Glasgow, Brook & Company
at 15 Wilton Avenue
TORONTO, CANADA